D1603945

Letters to Ann

The Korean War 1950–1951

Edited by Ann Marie

Letters to Ann

Published in the USA by:
Ann Marie
Denver, CO 80246
annmarie83@mac.com

ISBN 978-0-9893788-0-2

Printed in the United States of America.

Book and cover design by Darlene and Dan Swanson of Van-garde Imagery, Inc.

Preface

As the real Ann in this story used to say, there are just too many "Anns" in our family. I am not the "Ann" to whom the letters were sent. That was Ann Isabel Hughes, who was the daughter of Mary Lydia and John Francis Hughes. She was nearing her fourth birthday when she first started to receive notes and drawings from her father while he served in the Korean War.

Ann Isabel Hughes

Ann gave me copies of the letters after I became her sister-in-law in the 1980s. I loved the letters then, and continue to love them to this day. They are a uniquely unabridged snapshot of both a horrific and heroic time in American history.

Ann Marie, *Editor*

Contents

North Korea
invades
South Korea
at 4 a.m. on
Sunday, June 25, 1950.

The Letters

2 July

Dear Ann

This is how the little Japanese girls carry their little baby brothers -

Love

Daddy.

The 7th Medical Battalion was based at Camp Sendai, Honshu, Japan, operating hastily-left medical facilities, evacuating wounded from ships and planes and transporting them to trains and hospitals.

O'Hern, Capt. Robert S., "Annual Report of Army Medical Service Activities for the year 1950," 18 Jan. 1951, p. 1-2. Korean War Unit Histories. *U.S. Army Medical Department Office of Medical History*. Web. 22 Sept. 2012.

Aug 6.

Dear Ann

> **The first week in August found those units of the battalion which were still at Camp Sendai preparing for a move to the Camp Fuji Maneuver area. The battalion departed Camp Sendai on August 7, and within a week after arrival at Camp Fuji, was assembled as an entire battalion for the first time since its employment in Japan.**
>
> O'Hern, Capt. Robert S., "Annual Report of Army Medical Service Activities for the year 1950," 18 Jan. 1951, p. 2. Korean War Unit Histories. *U.S. Army Medical Department Office of Medical History*. Web. 22 Sept. 2012.

Little Japanese children's house was covered with river water which carried the house down the river. The children had to climb up on the roof so they wouldn't get wet. They thought it was so funny even though they didn't have a house any more. See the doggy swimming behind? He fell.

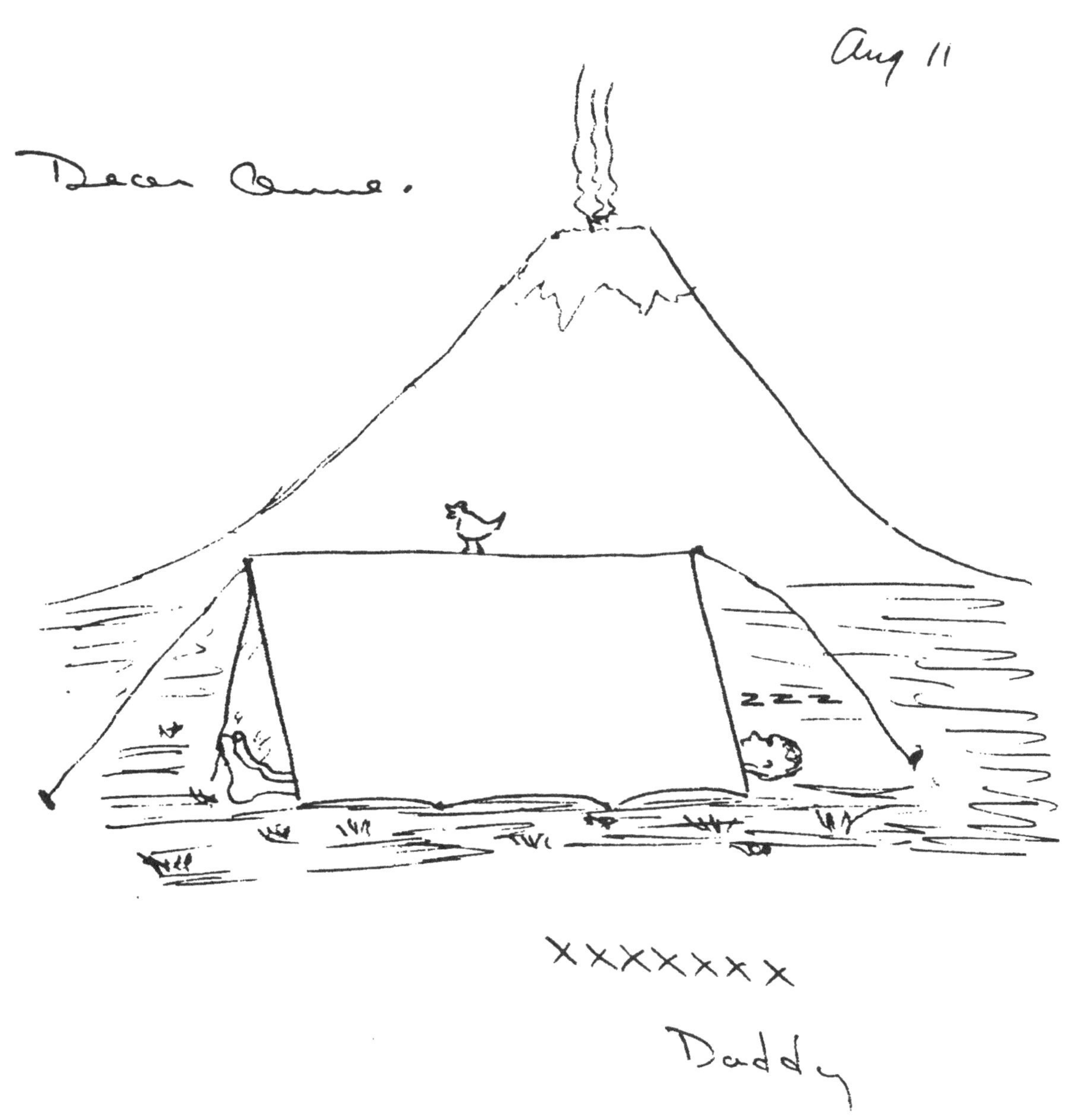

Aug 11

Dear Anne.

xxxxxxx

Daddy

"I was assigned as platoon leader of a clearing company and the first of August left for a barren stretch of volcanic ash at the base of Fujiyama and one month's preparation for the Korean offensive."

Capt. John F. Hughes, Letter to Springfield Hospital, 19 Oct. 1950.

A 16 hour a day training schedule was effected with physical and mental conditioning stressed. Road marches, day and night, at least four (4) times a week were taken. This strenuous routine seven days a week continued throughout the remainder of the month.

O'Hern, Capt. Robert S., "Annual Report of Army Medical Service Activities for the year 1950," 18 Jan. 1951, p. 3. Korean War Unit Histories. *U.S. Army Medical Department Office of Medical History*. Web. 22 Sept. 2012.

Aug 13

Dear Ann —

I have got a sore foot + almost no hair,

Love
Daddy

Aug 21

Dear Ann --

I have a new car. It is called a jeep. It is like a Nash Rambler since it is a convertible. See the funny steel hat I wear.

Love Buddy

xxxxxxxxx

In these regions, human waste was turned into instant fertilizer which, in turn, created a pervasive smell which was, unfortunately, well-remembered by those who experienced it first hand.

Halberstam, David, *The Coldest Winter*, p. 271.

30 Aug

Dear Ann —

This is a honey wagon with honey buckets on top. The Japanese boy is carrying it out into the field to make the RICE grow better.

Daddy
XXXXXXXXXXX

Tell mama that the address she is using now IS CORRECT.

1 Sept

Dear Conn –

I have to shave using my steel hat to hold water in. My houseboy just saw this picture and thinks it is very funny too!

Love

Daddy.

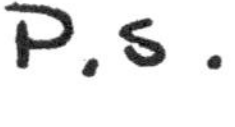

P.S.

I have a bathroom that is outside + made of wood.

Sept 5

Dear Ann -

The wind blew so hard the other day it blew my tent away while I was asleep. It landed right on top of the mountain.

Love Daddy
xxxxxxxxxxx

Sept 6

Dear Ann —

THERE ARE BIG EAGLES HERE. THEY COME CLOSE TO US AND TRY TO STEAL OUR FOOD BUT WE SCARE THEM AWAY.

LOVE

Daddy

XXXXXXX

Sept 6

This is the tower we climbed on top of and you had to hold on tight so you wouldn't fall.

On 7 September, the battalion departed by rail from Camp Fuji for the Yokohama Port of Embarkation to board the USNS General Randall.

O'Hern, Capt. Robert S., "Annual Report of Army Medical Service Activities for the year 1950," 18 Jan. 1951, p. 3. Korean War Unit Histories. *U.S. Army Medical Department Office of Medical History*. Web. 22 Sept. 2012.

Sept 1950

Dear Ann -

I have 4 big trucks to carry my tents in and a trailer behind to carry water in. I don't have any elephants to help me put up my tents like the circus does,

Love
Daddy

Water supply was especially important because most of the available Korean sources were contaminated.

Cowdrey, Albert, *The Medics' War*, p. 137.

9 Sept

Dear Ann –

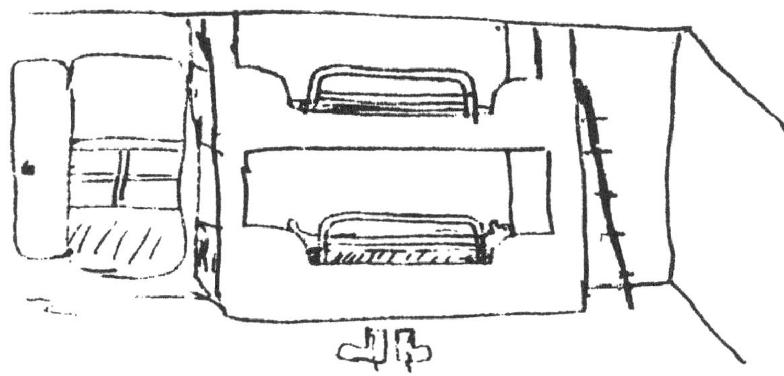

I sleep on a bed with a Rail on it so that when the boat Rocks I don't fall out of bed. Another Pappasan (that is Japanese For Daddy) sleeps above ME and has to climb the ladder to get into bed.

Love
Daddy
XXXXXX

P.S.

If you are a good girl – someday we will take a Boat to Japan and climb Mt. Fuji. O.K?

That's us.

The ship sailed at 0500 11 September. After the ship was out on the high seas, the staff and company commanders were informed they were to take part in "Operation Goldrush" - the invasion of Inchon on September 15.

O'Hern, Capt. Robert S., "Annual Report of Army Medical Service Activities for the year 1950," 18 Jan. 1951, p. 3. Korean War Unit Histories. *U.S. Army Medical Department Office of Medical History.* Web. 22 Sept. 2012.

General Douglas MacArthur initiates a surprise amphibious landing behind North Korean lines at the Port of Inchon on September 15, 1950.

Inchon Harbor, Sept.15, 1950, U.S. Navy

The voyage was uneventful and the ship arrived at Inchon Harbor on 16 September.

O'Hern, Capt. Robert S., "Annual Report of Army Medical Service Activities for the year 1950," 18 Jan. 1951, p. 3. Korean War Unit Histories. *U.S. Army Medical Department Office of Medical History*. Web. 22 Sept. 2012.

LSTs on "Yellow Beach," Inchon, Sept.16, 1950, U.S. Navy

The unit debarked on September 19, 1950.

O'Hern, Capt. Robert S., "Annual Report of Army Medical Service Activities for the year 1950," 18 Jan. 1951, p. 3. Korean War Unit Histories. *U.S. Army Medical Department Office of Medical History*. Web. 22 Sept. 2012.

After nightfall on 19th September, the 7th Medical Battalion came ashore on LSTs at Yellow Beach, the divisional landing area. Marching through darkness to an assembly point, the men bedded down in abandoned buildings to await their equipment. But the Inchon tides intervened; three days elapsed before the battalion's vehicles were unloaded.

Cowdrey, Albert, *The Medics' War*, p. 101.

Sept. 22

Dear Ann -

We give the poor little Korean children some of our food to eat.

WE give the big KOREAN CHILDREN A KICK IN THE SEAT BECAUSE they ARE BAD CHILDREN AND STEAL OUR THINGS.

Ann and "Peach"

Dear Ann -

This is the dentist cleaning your teeth while mamma sits in the chair with her tooth ache.

Love
Daddy
xxxxxx

28 Sept

Dear Ann -

In Korea the men wear clothes like this

The women like this

Big children like this

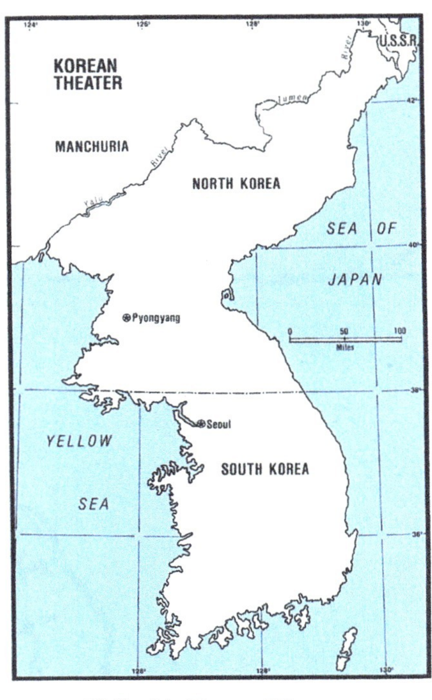

U.S. Air Force History and Museums Program

Korea is about the size of Utah and, in shape, resembles Florida.

Appleman, Roy E., *South to the Naktong, North to the Yalu (June-November 1950)*, p. 0011. koreanwar2.org. Web. 17 Jan. 2013.

and little children like this —

29 Sept 50

Medical units in Korea often set up in pre-existing buildings such as schools.

Cowdrey, Albert,
The Medics' War,
pp. 76, 77, 79, 83, 101.

The children try to come to school but I have to send them home since I am using their school house for my hospital.

Love
Daddy
xxxxx

Tell your mother I got her letter from the 29th. I am doing fine but awfully busy. Will write again to her soon.

Love
Daddy

In late September of 1950,
U.S. Marines drive
enemy forces away
from the South Korean
capital of Seoul.

The battle for Seoul was a period when I was very busy since, beside army casualties, we cared for over a thousand civilians who had been injured. No other medical care was available to these people at that time.

Capt. John F. Hughes, Letter to Springfield Hospital, 19 Oct. 1950.

Seoul 1950, Capt. F. L. Scheiber, U.S. Army

"Every large brick or concrete building in Seoul was either completely destroyed or damaged to the point of uselessness. The largest residential sections were burned out completely and one could hardly get into or out of the city because of the thousands of refugees. Yet, the day after the city had fallen, I walked down 'Black Market Street' and for over a mile you could buy American cigarettes, cameras, film, beer, Scotch whiskey and any other item that is scarce for us to get thru any other channel, at hundreds of makeshift stalls along the road."

Capt. John F. Hughes, Letter to Springfield Hospital, 19 Oct. 1950.

The enemy was indifferent to the Western etiquette of war. Attacks on medical personnel, vehicles and tents became the rule rather than the exception.

Cowdrey, Albert, *The Medics' War*, p. 75.

Section V

AWARD OF THE BRONZE STAR MEDAL.—By direction of the President, under the provisions of Executive Order 9419, 4 February 1944 (Sec II, WD Bul 3, 1944), and pursuant to authority contained in AR 600-45, the Bronze Star Medal with "V" device for heroic achievement in connection with military operations against an armed enemy of the United States is awarded to the following named officers and enlisted men:

CAPTAIN JOHN F. HUGHES, O-9[illegible]6456, Medical Corps, United States Army, Clearing Company, 7th Medical Battalion, distinguished himself by heroic action in the vicinity of Onchon-Ni, Korea, on 9 October 1950. On this date, a division convoy, enroute to Pusan, Korea, was ambushed and prevented from proceeding. Casualties consisted of six killed and twelve wounded in action. Without regard for his personal safety, Captain Hughes voluntarily advanced to a position approximately one thousand yards forward of the nearest friendly troops and, under heavy enemy fire and constant observation, administered medical care to the wounded men. Upon arrival of litter bearers, Captain Hughes proceeded further forward to two casualties in the immediate area of the enemy. After directing cover fire upon the enemy, he succeeded in treating and evacuating the two wounded men. The heroism displayed by Captain Hughes on this occasion reflects great credit on himself and the military service. Entered the military service from the State of Massachusetts.

The battalion and the attached 1st Mobile Army Surgical Hospital (MASH) departed for Pusan, Korea on October 8. The convoy was ambushed en-route and suffered several casualties. Heroic efforts on the part of members of the battalion in rescue and care of the wounded resulted in one officer being awarded the Bronze Star Medal with "V" device for valor.

O'Hern, Capt. Robert S., "Annual Report of Army Medical Service Activities for the year 1950," 18 Jan. 1951, p. 4. Korean War Unit Histories. *U.S. Army Medical Department Office of Medical History.* Web. 22 Sept. 2012.

The unit arrived at Pusan on the 10th of October and bivouacked outside the city.

O'Hern, Capt. Robert S., "Annual Report of Army Medical Service Activities for the year 1950," 18 Jan. 1951, p. 4. Korean War Unit Histories. *U.S. Army Medical Department Office of Medical History*. Web. 22 Sept. 2012.

I HAVE A PIG AS A PET NOW. HE RIDES IN MY TRAILER.

Dear Ann:

Little girls stand by the ROAD + SELL APPLES AS I DRIVE BY IN MY JEEP. THE APPLES HAVE WORMS IN THEM.

LOVE Daddy
XXXXX

The little children come out in SMALL BOATS with a Big paddle in the back to our SHIPS. WE throw FOOD over to THEM.

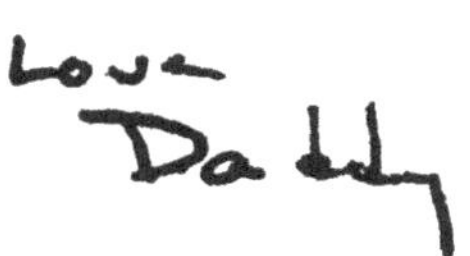

The battalion, less two platoons, departed Pusan aboard the USNS General E. D. Patrick on October 16, 1950.

O'Hern, Capt. Robert S., "Annual Report of Army Medical Service Activities for the year 1950," 18 Jan. 1951, p. 4. Korean War Unit Histories. *U.S. Army Medical Department Office of Medical History*. Web. 22 Sept. 2012.

Oct 18

Dear Ann—

I stand on two boxes AND TWO LITTLE Boys polish my boots FOR A PIECE OF CANDY.

P.S.

It RAINED so HARD THE OTHER NIGHT I FLOATED RIGHT OUT OF MY TENT IN my sleeping bag.

Love
Daddy
xxxxx

Under cover of darkness, Chinese troops begin to cross the Yalu River into North Korea on October 19, 1950. They are skilled in camouflage.

Chinese Forces Cross the Yalu River, Li Min, PLA Daily, 1951, Issue 4

20 Oct

Dear Ann -

My boys sneaked dogs, pigs, and rabbits onto the ship without any one seeing them. The Captain found them and got very mad. They may even have sneaked little Korean children on but no one has found them yet.

The sailing of the convoys was delayed for about two weeks because the Wonsan Harbor destination was still being cleared of mine fields.

Appleman, Roy E., *South to the Naktong, North to the Yalu (June-November 1950)*, p. 0485. koreanwar2. org. Web. 17 Jan. 2013.

Oct 22

Dear Ann -

You take good care of my car while I am gone. Polish it, scrub it, and make it shine. I don't want you wetting your pants in the back seat either.

Love

Daddy.

XXXXX

The 7th Division was ultimately diverted to Iwon, a coastal town far to the north. From there, the division was to strike over "a poor dirt road that twisted its way through the mountains and the Korean upland" to Hyesanjin on the Manchurian border.

Cowdrey, Albert,
The Medics' War, p. 112-13.

Oct 23

Dear Ann -

Extensive training was given in the use of cold weather clothing and precautions in prevention of cold injury.

O'Hern, Capt. Robert S., "Annual Report of Army Medical Service Activities for the year 1950," 18 Jan. 1951, p. 4. Korean War Unit Histories. *U.S. Army Medical Department Office of Medical History*. Web. 22 Sept. 2012.

I got new winter clothes the other day. They are all white so you can't see me in the snow. I have a snow jacket just like yours with a hood and fur on it. See my big boots. I also got glasses with fur around the edges so my eyes won't get cold.

Love
Daddy
xxxxx

In hopes of ending operations before the onset of winter, General MacArthur orders his ground commanders on October 24 to advance to the northern border with all available forces and as rapidly as possible. The consequences are devastating.

Oct 25

Dear Ann

LITTLE GIRLS IN KOREA SELL APPLES TO THE SOLDIERS WITH THEIR BABY BROTHERS STRAPPED ONTO THEIR BACKS.

LOVE
Daddy
XXXXX

"LST" stands for Landing Ship, Tank. It was the military designation for naval vessels created during WW II to support amphibious operations. The ships could carry a significant quantity of vehicles, cargo and troops directly onto unimproved shores.

"LST" definition, *encyclopedia.thefreedictionary.com.* Web. 19 March 2013.

Oct 29

Dear Ann

WE TRAVELLED ON A BOAT WITH BIG DOORS ON THE FRONT WHICH OPEN UP SO I CAN DRIVE MY JEEP OFF.

Because the open beaches were wholly at the mercy of the weather and high seas, the unloading of the 7th Infantry Division at Iwon went forward slowly. When it was completed, the Division's total strength would exceed 26,600 men.

Appleman, Roy E., *South to the Naktong, North to the Yalu (June-November 1950)*, p. 0561. koreanwar2.org. Web. 17 Jan. 2013.

Oct 31

Dear Ann

There are big bears here in Northern Korea, just like you Saw in the Circus. They can't do any tricks though.

Love
Daddy
XXXXX

Nov. 7

Dear Ann –

I flew over some mountains in a little airplane.

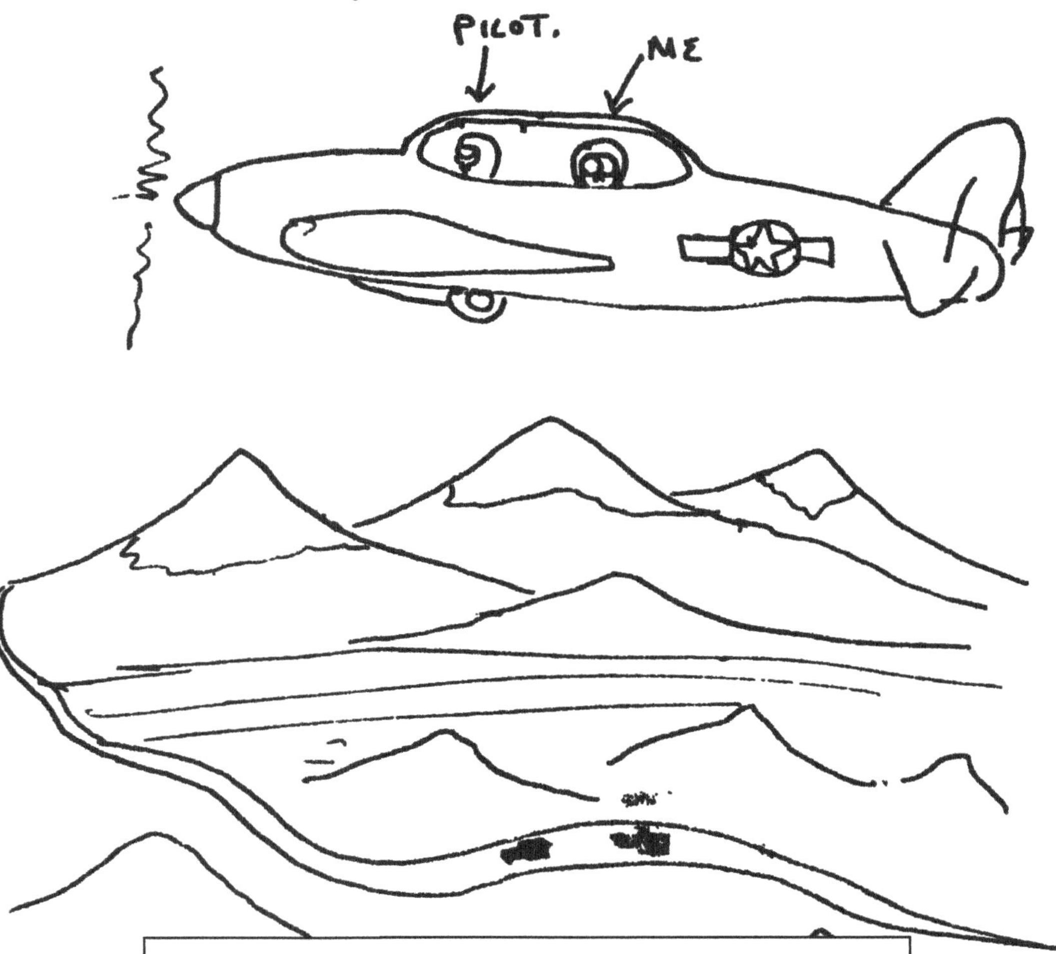

T–6 trainer aircraft were used in Korea. Because their call sign was "Mosquito," they soon became known in Army and Air Force parlance as "Mosquitoes." Each plane normally carried an Air Force pilot and a ground force observer.

Appleman, Roy E., *South to the Naktong, North to the Yalu (June-November 1950)*, p. 0078. koreanwar2.org. Web. 17 Jan. 2013.

Nov 14

Dear Brian

JOE DIMAGGIO CAME TO SEE ME AND THE SICK ~~SHOULDER~~ SOLDIERS TODAY.

Love
Daddy
XXXXX

Joe DiMaggio 1951
Baseball Digest

16 Nov.

Dear Ann

Little children don't have seats in their pants in Korea. Saves wearing diapers

Love
Daddy
xxxxx

Nov. 18

Dear Ann -

Did you AND David play Nice?

OR

Did you Fight?

Daddy

Nov. 20

Dear [illegible]

The area to the north of the North Korean capital of Pyongyang was called Tiger Country by the Koreans, presumably because tigers once had actually lived there.

Halberstam, David, *The Coldest Winter,* p. 396-97.

M-1 rifles and .45 caliber pistols were drawn and issued to the officers and enlisted men.

O'Hern, Capt. Robert S., "Annual Report of Army Medical Service Activities for the year 1950," 18 Jan. 1951, p. 7. Korean War Unit Histories. *U.S. Army Medical Department Office of Medical History.* Web. 22 Sept. 2012.

I HAVE A NEW TIGER SKIN HAT. IT IS VERY WARM. SEE HOW I TIE MY MITTENS ON JUST LIKE YOU DO? I ALSO HAVE A PISTOL UNDER MY SHOULDER JUST LIKE GANGSTERS WEAR.

LOVE
DADDY
x xxxx

Dear Ann Nov 24

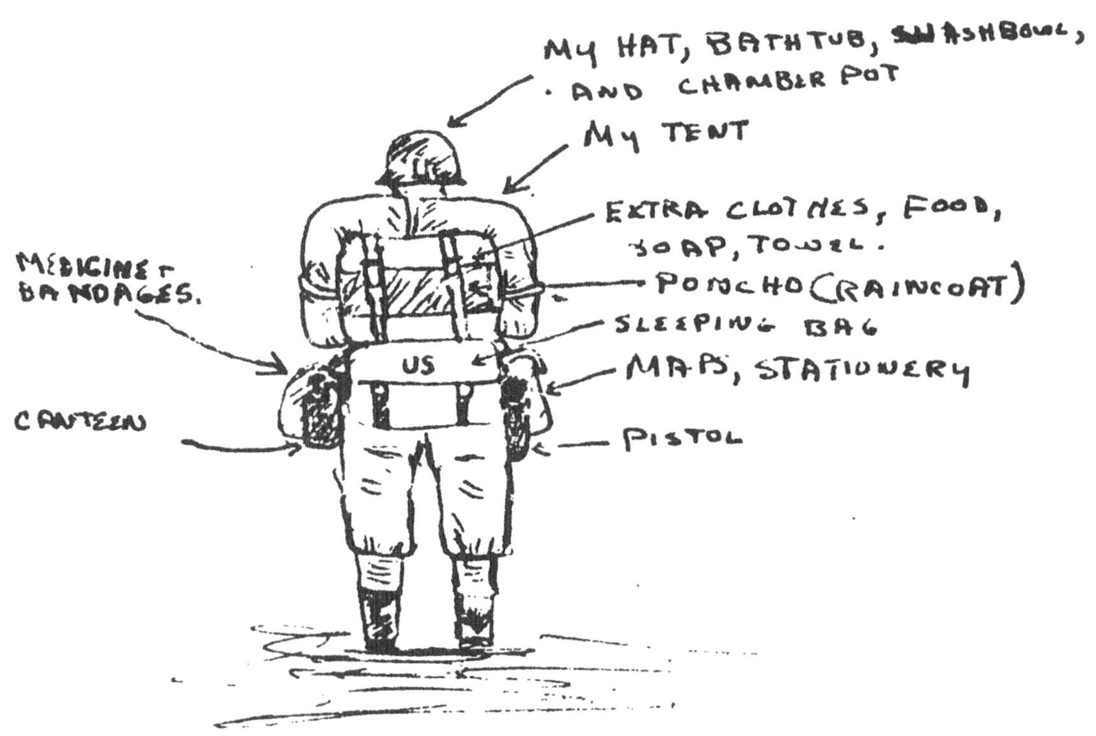

THIS IS HOW I LOOK WHEN I GET OFF BOATS. I CARRY EVERYTHING I NEED ON MY BACK. IT WEIGHS ABOUT 3 TIMES WHAT YOU DO.

LOVE

DADDY

The "Home-by-Christmas" UN Offensive launches on November 24, 1950 but the Chinese are waiting in ambush.

"Korean War Timeline," *authentichistory.com.*, last modified July 17, 2012. Web. 23 Sept. 2012.

The Chinese attack en masse on the night of November 25, 1950. The war takes on a horrific new dimension as 180,000 Chinese soldiers surround MacArthur's widely separated forces. 60,000 of those soldiers encircle the UN forces at Chosin Reservoir.

Marines at Chosin Reservoir, Dec.1950, U.S. Marine Corps

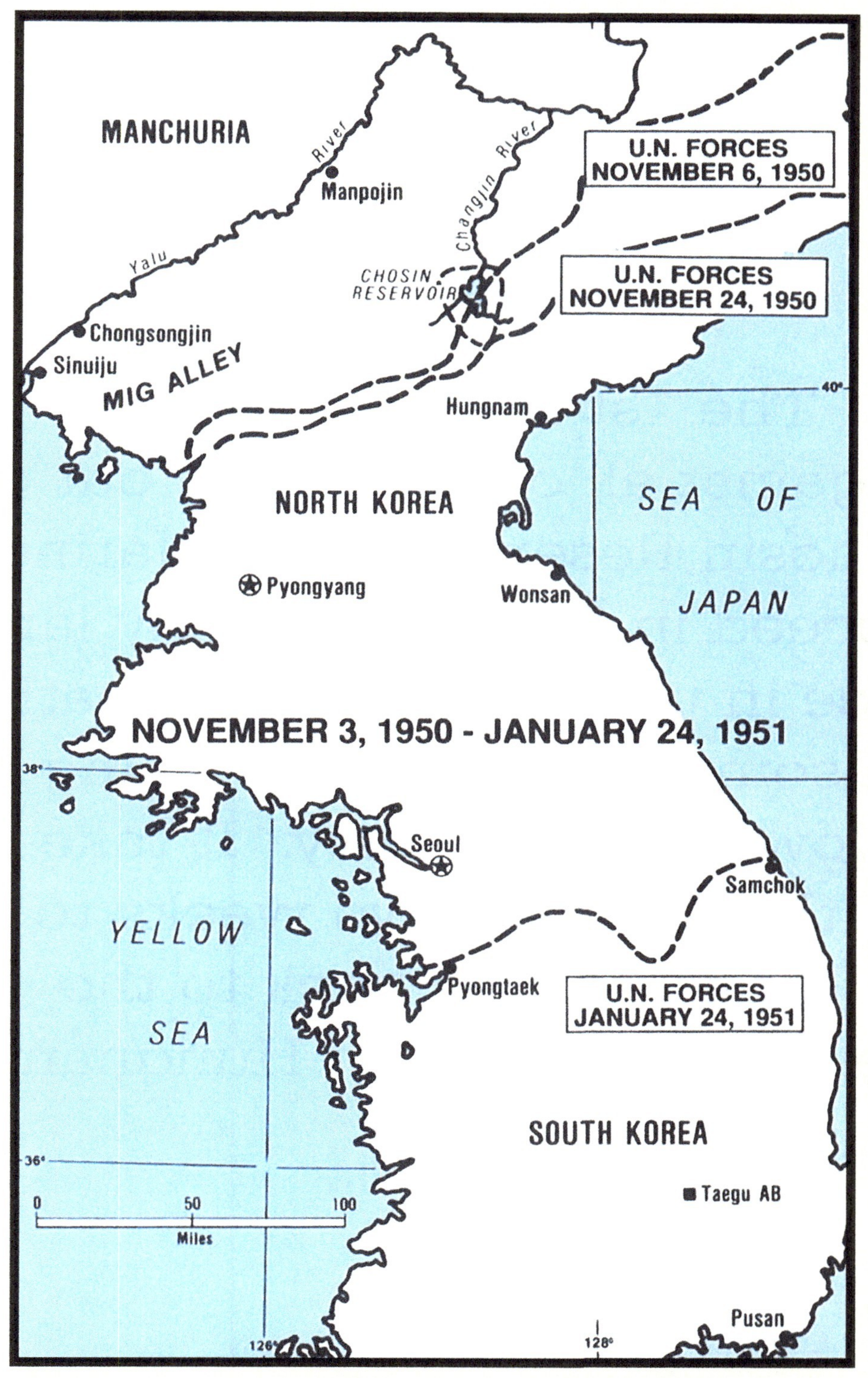

Endicott, Judy G., Ed., "The USAF in Korea," pamphlet, 2001. *Organizational History Branch Research Division, Air Force Historical Research Agency, Air Force History and Museums Program.* Web. Oct. 2012.

The 1st Marine Division, against all odds, breaks out of Chosin Reservoir. The Marines succeed in fighting a vastly larger force in unbearably cold weather, with some temperatures falling to as low as minus forty. It takes the Division two weeks to fight its way back to the evacuation port of Hungnam.

Dec 1

Dear Ann —

The battalion received orders to withdraw from Northeast Korea on 1 December. It moved by motor convoy to Hamhung.

O'Hern, Capt. Robert S., "Annual Report of Army Medical Service Activities for the year 1950," 18 Jan. 1951, p. 5. Korean War Unit Histories. *U.S. Army Medical Department Office of Medical History*. Web. 22 Sept. 2012.

THAT PICTURE OF YOU WITH YOUR SUIT ON AND YOUR FUNNY FACE SCARED ME!

LOVE

DADDY

XXXXX!

In the 7th Division, the medical platoon at Hargaru-ri had nearly four hundred patients when they were ordered to "make a break for it."

Ginn, Col. Richard V. N., *The History of the U.S. Army Medical Service Corps*, 1997, p. 235. history.amedd.army.mil. Web. 23 Sept. 2012.

While in Hamhung, the battalion assisted in caring for the wounded coming in from the Chosin Reservoir area.

O'Hern, Capt. Robert S., "Annual Report of Army Medical Service Activities for the year 1950," 18 Jan. 1951, p. 5. Korean War Unit Histories. *U.S. Army Medical Department Office of Medical History.* Web. 22 Sept. 2012.

Chosin Reservoir Frostbite Casualties, Dec. 1950, U.S. National Archives

Dec.

Dear Ann –

THE CHINAMEN HERE WEAR PADDED COATS JUST LIKE A QUILT.

Love
Daddy.

The Chinese uniforms were heavily quilted cotton, usually a mustard brown color, although some of the Chinese soldiers wore dark blue. The quilted uniform was warm until it became water-soaked; then it was difficult to dry. The soldiers' faceless shoes were of cloth, low-cut, rubber-soled and worn with sets of cotton socks. Heavy cotton caps had ear flaps that gave neck protection.

Appleman, Roy E., *South to the Naktong, North to the Yalu (June-November 1950)*, p. 0525. koreanwar2.org. Web. 17 Jan. 2013.

MacArthur's army is now in a full-scale retreat over the cold and mountainous terrain of Korea. Called the "Big Bugout," it is the longest retreat in American war history.

The 7th Medical Battalion provided evacuation over a 230-mile route, in temperatures as low as -24° F.

Ginn, Col. Richard V.N., *The History of the U.S. Army Medical Service Corps*, 1997, p. 237. history.amedd.army.mil. Web. 23 Sept. 2012.

Dec. 7 1950

Dear Ann —

This is me and my trucks coming over the mountains. Boy, is it cold.

Love
Daddy
xxxxx

It was the Clearing Company's first experience in withdrawal tactics and support of this type of operation.

Miner, Capt. Richard L., "Command Report," Jan. 2, 1950 (sic), Command Report for the Month of December 1950, Inc. IV, Jan. 1951. Korean War Unit Histories. *U.S. Army Medical Department Office of Medical History*. Web. 1 Oct. 2012.

Dec 8

Dear Ann—

THIS IS YOU DRAWING PICTURES FOR ME WITH YOUR COOKIE CUTTER. But what's that puddle on the FLOOR. WAS A BIG DOG JUST THERE?

LOVE
Daddy

On 5 December, the 2nd Platoon left Pukchong and joined the rest of the company at Unhung-ni. A Clearing Station was in operation at this location until 15 December.

Miner, Capt. Richard L., "Command Report," Jan. 2, 1950 (sic), Command Report for the Month of December 1950, Inc. IV, Jan. 1951. Korean War Unit Histories. *U.S. Army Medical Department Office of Medical History*. Web. 1 Oct. 2012.

Due to the advance position of some elements of the 7th Infantry Division, they were supplied with one "Baldwin" airdrop.

O'Hern, Capt. Robert S., "Annual Report of Army Medical Service Activities for the year 1950," 18 Jan. 1951, p. 9. Korean War Unit Histories. *U.S. Army Medical Department Office of Medical History*. Web. 22 Sept. 2012.

Dec 12

Dear Ann –

AIRPLANES DROPPED
FOOD AND MEDICINE
ON PARACHUTES FOR
ME WHEN I WAS
WAY UP IN THE
MOUNTAINS.
LOVE
Daddy
XXXXX

Dec 12
Dear Ann
EVERY time the big gun would shoot it would pick me up in the AIR WHILE I WAS IN MY SLEEPING BAG AND BOUNCE ME ON THE GROUND.
LOVE
DADDY
XXXXX

The gun depicted by Captain Hughes appears to be a M41 Gorilla.

The howitzer was placed on a pedestal in the rear, surrounded by a thin shield. It was a good design, agile and simple to operate but offered little protection to the crew from the elements or enemy fire. A total of about 85 were built. It saw service in Korea.

"1945-54 U.S.A. M41 Howitzer Motor Carriage 'Gorilla'," *battletanks.com*. Web. 19 March 2013.

155-mm Howitzer, Korea, U.S. Army Signal Corps

Dec 17

Dear Ann-

The battalion was ordered to withdraw from the Hamhung area. It left on the 14th of December. The battalion boarded the USNS General Freeman with a destination of Pusan.

O'Hern, Capt. Robert S., "Annual Report of Army Medical Service Activities for the year 1950," 18 Jan. 1951, p. 5. Korean War Unit Histories. *U.S. Army Medical Department Office of Medical History.* Web. 22 Sept. 2012.

THEY took us out to the big ships in little boats AND THEN WE HAD TO CLIMB UP NETS TO GET IN THE BIG SHIPS.

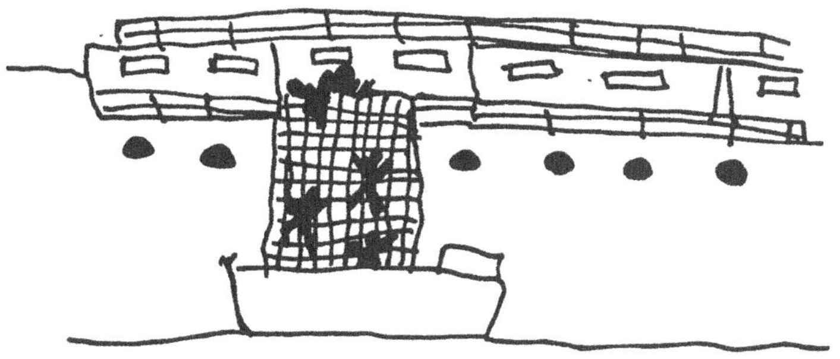

LOVE
Daddy
XXXXX

Dec 20

Dear Ann

WHILE I WAS LIVING IN THE CELLAR MY STOVE DIDN'T WORK RIGHT. ALL THE SMOKE CAME INTO THE ROOM, I GOT BLACK ALLOVER— ESPECIALLY MY HANDS + FACE (JUST LIKE YOU SOMETIMES)

LOVE
DADDY
XXXXX

When the battalion arrived at Pusan, they debarked and entrained for Toksong-dong, where a Division Clearing Station was established on December 20. The battalion remained at Toksong-dong for the remainder of the year.

O'Hern, Capt. Robert S., "Annual Report of Army Medical Service Activities for the year 1950," 18 Jan. 1951, p. 6. Korean War Unit Histories. *U.S. Army Medical Department Office of Medical History*. Web. 22 Sept. 2012.

Dec 23

Dear Ann

Santa had a difficult time coming down my chimney last night. My Xmas tree was decorated with beer can covers.

Love
Daddy
XXXXX

The buildings and physical set-up of the area were the finest ones the unit had moved into since arrival in Korea. The holidays were enjoyed immensely by all.

O'Hern, Capt. Robert S., "Annual Report of Army Medical Service Activities for the year 1950," 18 Jan. 1951, p. 6. Korean War Unit Histories. *U.S. Army Medical Department Office of Medical History.* Web. 22 Sept. 2012.

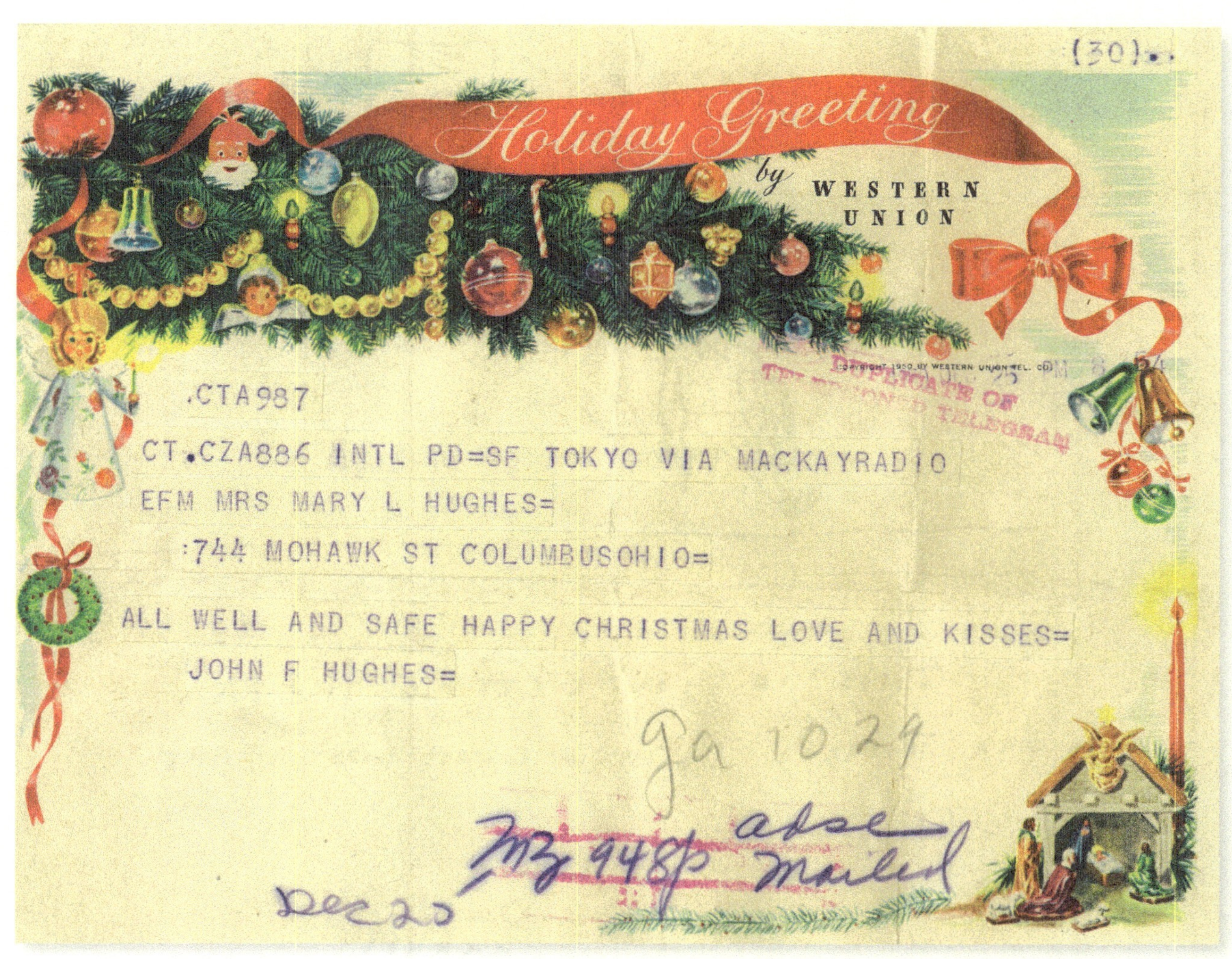
(30)..

Holiday Greeting by WESTERN UNION

.CTA987

CT.CZA886 INTL PD=SF TOKYO VIA MACKAYRADIO

EFM MRS MARY L HUGHES=

:744 MOHAWK ST COLUMBUSOHIO=

ALL WELL AND SAFE HAPPY CHRISTMAS LOVE AND KISSES=

JOHN F HUGHES=

Dec. 25

Dear Ann –

THIS IS YOU GETTING THE NEW YORK TIMES. DO YOU EVER LOSE PART OF IT?

LOVE
Daddy
XXXXX

Chinese forces cross the 38th parallel into South Korea on December 25, 1950.

Warnock, A. Timothy, Ed., "Air War Korea, 1950-53," *Air Force Association Online Journal*, Vol. 83, No. 10, Oct. 2000. Web. 25 Oct. 2012.

Lt. General Matthew Ridgway assumes command of the Eighth Army on December 26, 1950. He favors what comes to be known as the "meat grinder" approach. Each contact with the enemy would include every weapon available at the unit's disposal: infantry, armor, artillery and air.

Within Korea, the major means of moving large numbers of wounded remained the railways. Early hospital trains were improvised, consisting largely of converted boxcars and coaches, plus a few ancient hospital cars.

Cowdrey, Albert, *The Medics' War*, p. 149.

Dec. 27

Dear Ann –

I RODE ON AN OLD TRAIN WITH BROKEN WINDOWS. THE SMOKE WENT ALL THROUGH THE CARS FROM THE ENGINE.

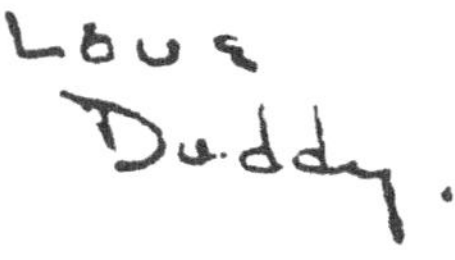

The Clearing Company admitted 750 patients in the month of December.

Miner, Capt. Richard L., "Command Report," Jan. 2, 1950 (sic), Command Report for the Month of December 1950, Inc. IV, Jan. 1951. Korean War Unit Histories. *U.S. Army Medical Department Office of Medical History*. Web. 1 Oct. 2012.

Almost half a million
Chinese and North Korean
troops launch a
new ground offensive
on January 1, 1951.

Jan 1, '51

Dear Ann

The 7th Infantry Division began its annual operations in the vicinity of Yongchon, Korea, which was a reassembly and training area.

Sellers, 1st Lt. Emmett L., "Annual Report of Medical Activities 1951," 9 Jan. 1952, p. 1. Korean War Unit Histories. *U.S. Army Medical Department Office of Medical History*. Web. 22 Sept. 2012.

I HEAR YOU ARE GOING TO TAKE DANCING LESSONS WITH OTHER LITTLE GIRLS

Love
Daddy

Jan 10

Dear Ann –

I MAKE WHISKEY FOR ALL THE BOYS OUT OF THE JUICE YOU SEND TO ME IN PACKAGES. THE WHISKEY IS CALLED "OLD ANNIE"

Love
DADDY
xxxxx

Jan 12

Dear Ann —

IT IS SO COLD HERE I GET ICICLES ON MY BEHIND EVEN SITTING BY THE FIRE.

LOVE

Daddy

XXXXX

The winter was harsh even by Korean standards. Temperatures rarely rose more than a few degrees above zero. Cold injuries were excessive.

Cowdrey, Albert, *The Medics' War*, p. 160.

Jan 15

Dear Ann –

I made an ice sled like the Koreans use and had one of the little Korean Boys push me on a frozen Rice Paddy.

Love
Daddy

Jan 17

Dear [illegible] —

I heard you got sick in your tummy the other night. Did mommy take good care of you?

Love
Daddy
[illegible]

Jan 21

Dear Ann -

I have a brand new jeep + trailer. My other jeep broke down so I traded it in.

Love
Daddy
xxxxx

The 7th Medical Battalion operated in combat status in support of the 7th Division throughout the year, operating a Clearing Company, an Ambulance and a Headquarters Company. Because of the type of terrain and the nature of the tactical situation, the Clearing Company maintained two clearing platoons in continuous operation and one clearing platoon in reserve and training status.

Sellers, 1st Lt. Emmett L., "Annual Report of Medical Activities 1951," 9 Jan. 1952, p. 2. Korean War Unit Histories. *U.S. Army Medical Department Office of Medical History*. Web. 22 Sept. 2012.

Jan 24

Dear Ann –

I heard FROM ONE OF THE ANGELS THE OTHER DAY THAT YOU SAY YOUR PRAYERS EVERY NIGHT.

LOVE
Daddy
xxxxx

Jan 26

Dear [illegible] –

EVERYBODY says you look like me.
IS THAT TRUE?

LOVE
DADDY
XXXX

After Yongchon, the 7th Infantry Division moved forward to the Chechon-Tanyang-Chungju area and launched its attack toward Pyongchang on January 26.

Sellers, 1st Lt. Emmett L., "Annual Report of Medical Activities 1951," 9 Jan. 1952, p. 1. Korean War Unit Histories. *U.S. Army Medical Department Office of Medical History.* Web. 22 Sept. 2012.

Though casualties exceeded all predictions, hospital death rates were the lowest in the history of warfare.

Cowdrey, Albert, *The Medics' War*, p. 141.

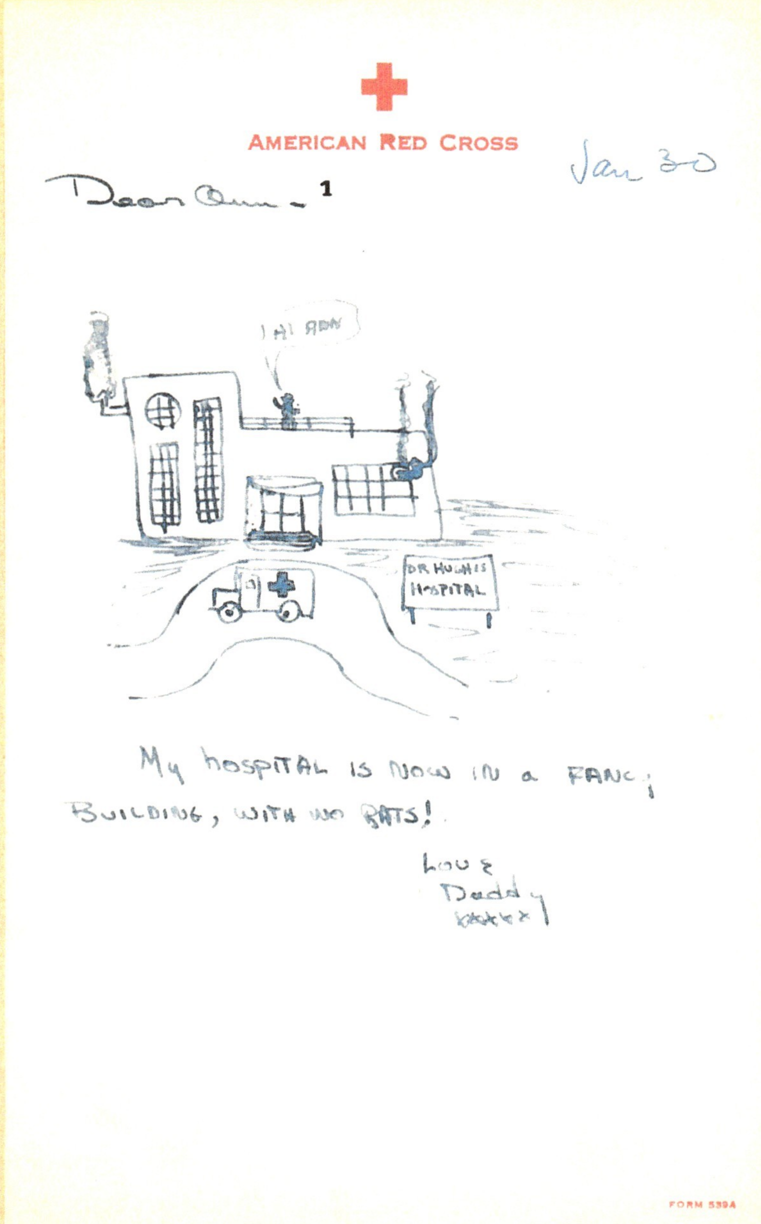

AMERICAN RED CROSS

Jan 30

Dear Ann -[1]

My hospital is now in a fancy building, with no rats!

Love &
Daddy
xxxxx

FORM 539A

1 This is a color copy of one of the original letters. It is one of the few that weathered loving young hands and the passage of time. The other letters used in this book are taken from photocopies which were made in the 1980s.

In January 1951, three Army helicopter detachments arrived in Korea with the mission of evacuating seriously wounded from the front lines. Each craft carried only a pilot and was equipped with two baskets or pods for litter patients.

Westover, John G., "Part V: Medical Corps," in *Combat Support in Korea*, Facsimile Reprint, 1987, 1990, p. 111. history.army.mil. Web. 15 Jan. 2013.

Jan 31

Dear Ann -

WE NOW HAVE A HELICOPTER TO TAKE
SICK SOLDIERS OVER THE MOUNTAINS. TWO
OF THEM ARE PUT
IN BASKETS
OUTSIDE THE
HELIOCOPTERS.

LOVE
Daddy
XXXXX

Bell H-13 Sioux Helicopter, Korea, 1950-51, Capt. John F. Hughes Photo

With all its remarkable implications for the future of Army medicine - indeed of emergency medicine, whether military or civilian - the rapid adoption of helicopter evacuation resulted from the nature of the Korean conflict and of the Korean countryside.

Cowdrey, Albert, *The Medics' War*, p. 95.

Feb 1

Dear Ann -

I hear you are getting so big and fat that you break all Nana's chairs when you sit down.

Love
Daddy
xxxxx

Feb 4

Dear Ann –

Road-rail buses with "flanged wheels raised" were used in Korea.

Cowdrey, Albert, *The Medics' War*, p. 181.

WE HAVE A BUS NOW THAT RUNS ON A RAILROAD TRACK TO TAKE THE SICK SOLDIERS TO THE HOSPITAL.

LOVE
DADDY
XXXXX

The two rail buses worked at night (when helicopters could not fly), were smooth and rapid in movement, carried more than twice as many men (250 in all) and allowed transfusions and other treatment to be given en route.

Cowdrey, Albert, *The Medics' War*, p. 179.

Feb 9

Dear Ann -

I gave my pigs to the zoo at PUSAN ~~[illegible]~~ so the KOREAN CHILDREN can SEE THEM. THEY ARE VERY LUCKY THEY AREN'T PORK CHOPS

LOVE
Daddy
xxxxx

Feb 13

Dear Ann:

OUR TRAIN WITH ALL OUR FOOD ON IT BLEW UP YESTERDAY. ALL WE HAVE LEFT TO EAT TODAY ARE CANDY BARS.

Trains were subject to ambushes and sniper attacks.

Ginn, Col. Richard V. N., *The History of the U.S. Army Medical Service Corps*, 1997, p. 239. history.amedd.army.mil. Web. 23 Sept. 2012.

Feb 13

Dear Ann.[2]

Received 4 letters from your mother yesterday and 3 packages, one of these from Mama. I guess burning down the post-office was one way of getting the mail out. We enjoyed the food you girls sent very much - all the boys wanted me to thank you.

We have been very busy the last 2 days. The Chinamen have attacked around Wonju[3] and we have had quite a few casualties coming through. I think we may be going South in a few days instead of north as we expected.

How do you like your dancing lessons? Are you a good dancer yet? I hope you got my valentine today. Give Momma a big kiss and have her give you one — right now. (Smack) OK?

For the fun of it I am going to take a correspondence course the army offers. It costs only two dollars. I think I will take one in Business Management.

By the way, I found out something the other day your old lady should know. If anything should happen to me

2 A transcription of this letter may be found immediately following the handwritten version.

3 Wonju was a bitter battle and it was uncertain as to who would emerge victorious until, quite literally, the final hours. The UN forces were hit so hard there that the area became known as Massacre Valley.

Halberstam, David, *The Coldest Winter*, p. 516.

For the fun of it I am going to take a correspondence course the army offers. It costs only two dollars. I think I will take one in Business Management.

By the way, I found out something the other day your old lady should know. If anything should happen to me she can apply to the Veteran's Administration and receive $130 per month for 6 mos. At the end of 6 mos she can get over $300 for you & her for the rest of her life since I am a reserve officer and come under the provisions of a Benefits Employment Commission (BEC) for Civil Service employees. She must apply for these benefits since they are not automatic. This is in addition to Life Insurance. If necessary - if anyone should ever turn her down it might be worth her while to see a lawyer & he would know how to go about it. I thought

I should tell her since many wives have no idea there is such a provision for reserve Officer's families.

Tell her too that I gave $10 for pictures to Sgt Woodstock our Battalion Sgt Major. His wife is going to send them.

By the way I got a new jacket and I won't let the rats get this one.

Well, little Sheba, be a good girl + say your prayers. Be nice to your sweet mummie so she doesn't have to be scolding you all the time.

I enjoyed the letters you wrote c̄ crayon very much. Do write some more, sweet child. I've got to draw a picture for your mother now.

Love
Daddy.

Transcription

Feb 13

Dear Ann -

Received 4 letters from your mother yesterday and 3 packages, one of those from Mama. I guess burning down the post-office was one way of getting the mail out. We enjoyed the food you girls sent very much - all the boys wanted me to thank you.

We have been very busy the last 2 days. The Chinamen have attacked around Wonju and we have had quite a few casualties coming through. I think we may have to go south in a few days instead of north as we expected.

How do you like your dancing lessons? Are you a good dancer yet? I hope you got my valentine today. Give momma a big kiss and have her give you one - right now. (Smack) Ok?

For the fun of it I am going to take a correspondence course the army offers. It costs only two dollars. I think I will take one in Business Management.

By the way, I found out something the other day your old lady should know. If anything should happen to me she can apply to the Veteran's Administration and receive $130 per month for 6 mos. At the end of 6 mos she can get over $300 for you and her for the rest of her life since I am a reserve officer and come under the provisions of a Benefits Employment Commission (BEC) for Civil Service employees. She must apply for these benefits since they are not automatic. This is in addition to Life Insurance. If necessary - if anyone should ever turn her down it might be worth her while to see a lawyer & he would know how to go about it. I thought I should tell her since many wives have no idea there is such a provision for reserve officer's families.

Tell her too that I gave $10 for pictures to Sgt Woodstock our Battalion Sgt Major. His wife is going to send them.

By the way I got a new jacket and I won't let the rats get this one.

Well, little Sheba, be a good girl & say your prayers. Be nice to your sweet mummie so she doesn't have to be scolding you all the time.

I enjoyed the letters you wrote [with] crayon very much. Do write some more, sweet child. I've got to draw a picture for your mother now.

Love,

Daddy.

Feb 18

Dear Ann -

Thank you for the nice
you wrote. How are your
lessons coming along. Do
you still wet your and
your . I hear you
have a new , called
Madeline. Is she the girl
that had her taken out.
Take good care of my and
my wife. Lots of xxxxx for you.

Love
Daddy.

Feb 22

Dear Ann

C-119 Flying Boxcar
U.S. Air Force

WE HAD BIG AIRPLANES DROP FOOD AND MEDICINES TO US WITH PARACHUTES. THEY JUST PUT THEIR NOSES UP IN THE AIR AND THE PARACHUTES SLIDE RIGHT OUT THE BACK.

LOVE
Daddy
xxxxx

Feb 26

Dear Ann

IT IS SO MUDDY IN MY TENT THAT I HAVE TO PUT MY COT UP ON A PLATFORM.

LOVE

DADDY
xxxxx

Housing conditions for troops and medical facilities have been fair under the very mobile combat conditions here in Korea. The housing consisted solely of bunkers and tents.

Sellers, 1st Lt. Emmett L., "Annual Report of Medical Activities 1951," 9 Jan. 1952, p. 4. Korean War Unit Histories. *U.S. Army Medical Department Office of Medical History.* Web. 22 Sept. 2012.

Feb 27

Dear Ann -

I received your letter yesterday. I am glad you like your dancing lessons. Do you have a new dancing dress? It is so muddy here now I have to wear big boots. The little Korean children have all gone down south for awhile. There is plenty of rice for them there so they will not be hungry. Give your mother a big kiss for me and have her give you two little ones

Love
Daddy.

When spring approached, the American ground troops in Korea experienced the misery of downpours of rain and sloshing through the mud.

"Weather Report-Korean War," *koreanwar-educator.org*. Web. 1 Oct. 2012.

Mar 4

Dear Ann –

IF Mamma (PEACHIE, that is) GETS HER HAND OPERATED ON, DON'T LET HER GET THE BANDAGE WET!

LOVE
DADDY
XXXXX

On March 14, 1951,
Operation Ripper
results in the successful
second recapture of Seoul.

Mar 16

Dear Ann -

Received a letter from your mother today dated Mar 9. I am glad her hand is getting better. Did she cry when she went to the hospital? I hope you are a good girl and help her around the house.

Those pictures of you and the young Leonard boy were very nice. You look nice & fat. Good enough to eat. I'll bet you would taste like roast beef. Have Mother taste you & tell us. Your mother looks nice & slim. I am glad ~~you~~ she is not getting fat.

It is getting warm here now. I have taken

off my fur hat and my long underwear.

Korea, 1950-51, Capt. John F. Hughes Photo

I may be going to Japan next month for awhile. There is lots of good rumors about that

Well, little sweetheart, be a good girl. Give your mother a big wet kiss and have her give you one.

Love
Daddy
xxxxx

2 April

Dear Ann –

I had a very nice hotel room. In Japan everyone sits, eats and sleeps on the floor.

World War II statistics showed that there were sharp increases in casualty rates of all types when troops experienced combat for more than 180 days without relief. Based on those statistics, the Department of the Army authorized temporary duty in Japan for the purpose of rest and recuperation (R&R) for their Korean troops.

Cowdrey, Albert, *The Medics' War*, p. 156.

3 April

Dear Ann

When I come home. I will teach you to fly a kite. O.K.?

Love
Daddy
xxxxx

6 April

Dear Ann –

I HAVE A NEW HAT I BOUGHT IN JAPAN AND A NEW VEST. THE HAT HAS SUN GLASSES ON IT. WHEN I TRAVEL EVERYONE WONDERS WHAT ARMY I'M IN.

LOVE
DADDY.

April 10

Dear Ann

I hope I RECOGNIZE YOU AND PEACHIE WHEN I GET HOME.

LOVE
Daddy.

President Harry S. Truman
recalls General MacArthur
on April 11, 1951.
General Ridgway takes over.

April 11

Dear Ann –

I have to do my own LAUNDRY IN AN old tin can NOW. I STIR THE CLOTHES WITH AN OLD STICK.

Love
Daddy
XXXXX

April 13

Dear Ann –

ARE YOU helping YOUR MOTHER PAINT THE HOUSE?

No

Dear Ann-

THE PEOPLE THAT MAKE TIDE WROTE TO ME AND TOLD ME YOW WERE USING TOO MUCH. I TOLD THEM YOU CAN USE AS MUCH AS YOO WANT.

LOVE
DADDY
XXXXX

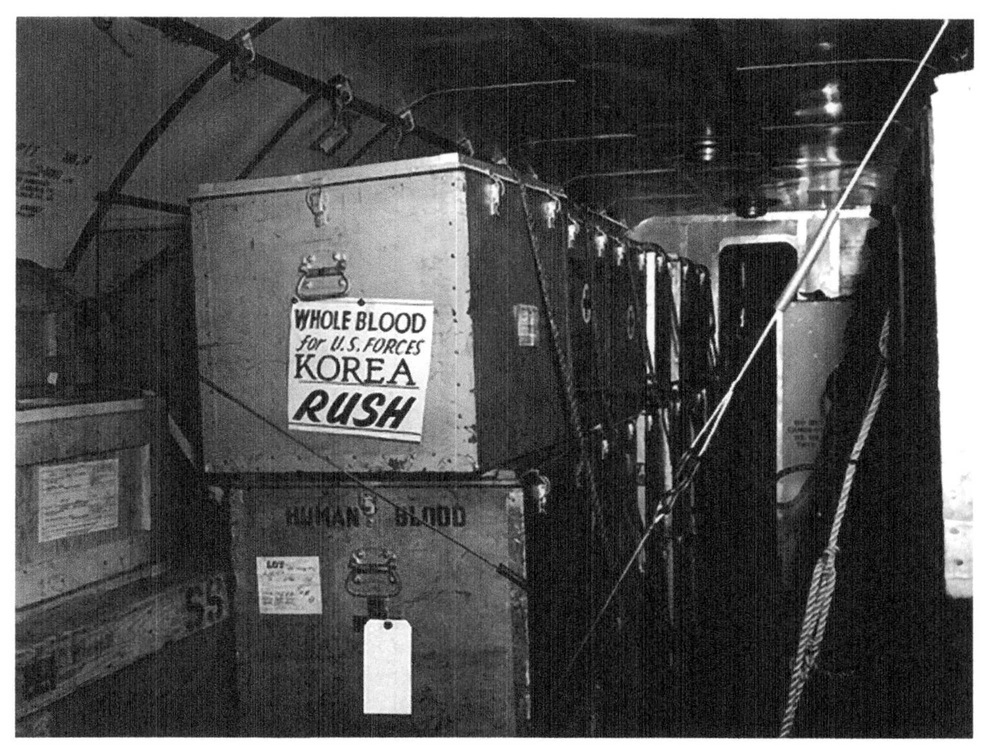

Whole Blood Rush, U.S. Army Korea (Historical Image Archive)

April 18

Dear Annie –

A key to the high Korean survival rates among the wounded, whole blood was especially important during the critical first hours of treatment. Most wounded men bled and the condition known as shock could rapidly become irreversible, ending in death. To halt the circulatory failure that was a consequence of hemorrhage and the basic factor in shock, whole blood had no equal.

Cowdrey, Albert, *The Medics' War*, p. 155.

Do you keep boxes of blood on a shelf in case you run out?

No

Love
Daddy
xxxxx

April 20

Dear Ann—

WE HAVE A BRIDGE THAT IS MADE OUT OF BARRELS BECAUSE THE OTHER BRIDGE BLEW UP.

LOVE
Daddy
XXXXX

Pontoon Bridge, Korea, 1950-51, Capt. John F. Hughes Photo

China's Spring Offensive
begins on April 22, 1951.
It is repelled.

April 23

Dear Ann—

I was so terribly, terribly pleased to receive your lovely letter on your very distinctive stationery. Take good care of your dear mother. You write very well for such a little girl. I liked your kisses very much. My but they were wet. I had to wring the paper out

Love

Daddy

XXXXX

April 25

7TH INFANTRY DIVISION

Dear Ann -

we have movies outside - just like a drive-in movies.

In medical units, frequent movies and increasing stocks of athletic equipment helped to pass the time between battles.

Cowdrey, Albert, *The Medics' War*, p. 183.

April 28

Dear Ann -

ARE YOUR BALLOONS STILL BREAKING ALL THE TIME?

LOVE

Daddy

xxxxx

April 30

Dear Ann –

WE had a little KOREAN GIRL IN MY HOSPITAL THAT DIDN'T HAVE ANY CLOTHES. SO I gave hER MY UNDERSHIRT AND IT HUNG DOWN TO THE GROUND.

LOVE
Daddy

May 5

Dear Ann.

Railroad Hand Cart, Korea, 1950-51,
Capt. John F. Hughes Photo

WE have a hand car we use TO RIDE FROM MY TENT DOWN TO DINNER. WE live Right NEXT TO the RailROAD Tracks.

Love,
Daddy
xxxxx

May 6

Dear Ann —

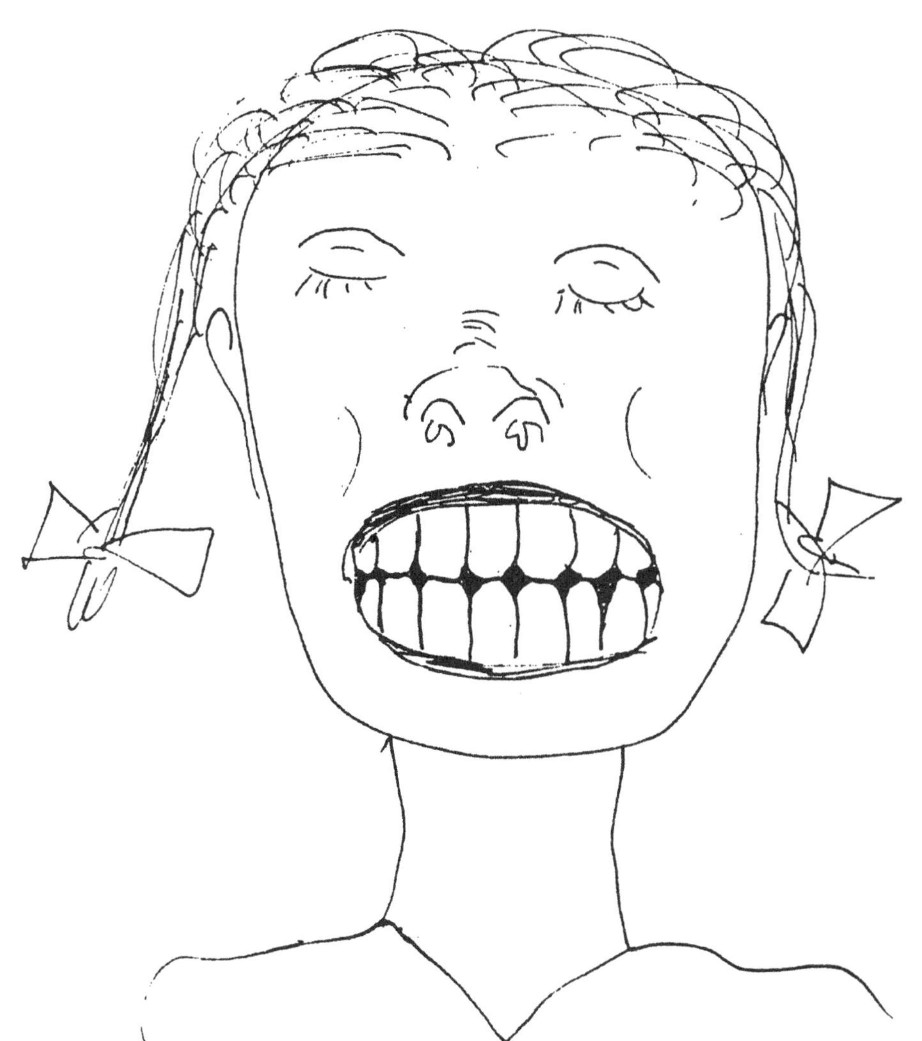

I HEAR YOU HAVE VERY NICE TEETH.

LOVE
Daddy
XXXXX

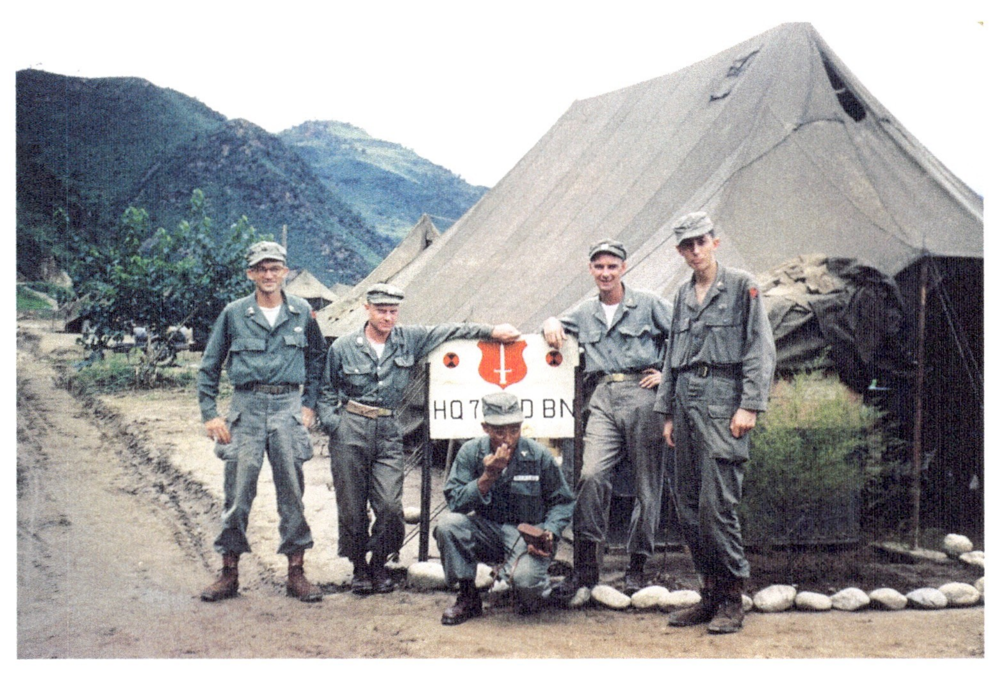

HQ 7th Medical Battalion, Capt. John F. Hughes (second from the right), Korea, 1950-51

A clearing company is an organization consisting of one or more clearing stations, company headquarters and clearing platoons. Tasks include reception, the sorting and temporary shelter of battle casualties and appropriate treatment for either return to their units or transfer of the seriously injured further to the rear.

"Clearing company" definition, *medical-dictionary.thefreedictionary.com*. Web. 1 Oct. 2012.

Clearing Station, The Korean War, Historical Art Work,
U.S. Army Medical Department Office of Medical History

Photos Courtesy of Doug Halbert

Standard operating procedures dictated that the two clearing platoons of each clearing company would leapfrog each other to keep up with the tempo of battle. As one platoon set up and operated a clearing station, the other would displace to a new location, and, when the second was operational, the first would shut down and relocate. It was an exhausting regimen.

Ginn, Col. Richard V. N., *The History of the U.S. Army Medical Service Corps*, 1997, p. 237. history.amedd.army.mil. Web. 23 Sept. 2012.

CLEARING COMPANY
7TH MEDICAL BATTALION
APO 7 C/O PM SAN FRANCISCO, CALIFORNIA

Dear Ann –

I am sending you some from a . We didn't have any and were so hungry. So we took our and him. Now we have and we aren't hungry any more. I am sending you some . You can put them in your . Be a good girl and don't . Give sweet PEACH a big

LOVE
Daddy
XXXXX

May 9

Dear Ann -

All the CHILDREN ARE HELPING THEIR DADDY's plant Rice IN THE Paddies

Love

Daddy

xxxxx

Korea was both beautiful and sordid. The green hills and patchwork-patterned rice paddies had an enchanting beauty when seen from a distance.

Appleman, Roy E., *South to the Naktong, North to the Yalu*, p. 0006. koreanwar2.org. Web. 17 Jan. 2013.

Rice Paddies, Korea, 1950-51, Capt. John F. Hughes Photo

May 11

Dear Ann—

I did a great big washing today.

Love
Daddy
xxxxx

CLEARING COMPANY
7TH MEDICAL BATTALION
APO 7 C/O PM SAN FRANCISCO, CALIFORNIA

Dear Ginnie —

May 22

I hope you are being a good girl

Love
Daddy
XXXX+

CLEARING COMPANY
7TH MEDICAL BATTALION
APO 7 C/O PM SAN FRANCISCO, CALIFORNIA

Dear Ann—

I am much diasapointed in you. The fairies tell me you are still wetting your pants. I do not like little girls who do this. They smell. If you are my girl you will not do this. Do you understand!!!!!. You tell your mother when you have to go while you are in . While you are playing , you in the house S̄ being told. Sit on the pot by yourself.

Daddy

(No kisses you little pants soiler)

CLEARING COMPANY
7TH MEDICAL BATTALION
APO 7 C/O PM SAN FRANCISCO, CALIFORNIA

May 22

My dearest Ann—

Enclosed I am sending you some pictures of me of where I live. I am moving my tent in a few days. I like to travel so much. I am also sending a surrender leaflet we drop to the Chinese. When you finish looking at it you might give it to your older cousin whose name is Scott Martin. Have you met him yet? Tell your sweet mother I may send a box of clothes home in the next few weeks. I'll let her know when I ship it. Give her a long wet kiss from me & have her give you one if you have any handy. Be a good non-pants-wetting girl

Love & kisses
Daddy
xxxxx

"Officers Quarters," Capt. John F. Hughes, Korea, 1951

CLEARING COMPANY
7TH MEDICAL BATTALION
APO 7 C/O PM SAN FRANCISCO, CALIFORNIA

May, 24

Dear Ann -

I understand you like to play with worms when you help your mother in the garden.

Love
Daddy
XXXX

CLEARING COMPANY
7TH MEDICAL BATTALION
APO 7 C/O PM SAN FRANCISCO, CALIFORNIA

30 May 51

Dear Annie ——

Received your very nice letter today
Don't let your mother lose any more of
your sox — after all they cost good
money. It has been raining all day
today. I have a raincoat that covers
ME like a table cloth.
IT has no sleeves in it.

Love
Daddy
XXXXX

Summers are hot and humid in Korea, with a monsoon season generally lasting from June to September.

Appleman, Roy. E., *South to the Naktong, North to the Yalu*, p. 0012.
koreanwar2.org. Web. 17 Jan. 2013.

By June of 1951, General Ridgway leads the UN forces back to the 38th Parallel. Battle lines stabilize at that position.

CLEARING COMPANY
7TH MEDICAL BATTALION
APO 7 C/O PM SAN FRANCISCO, CALIFORNIA

June 2, 1951

Dear Ann -

I have sent a to you + PEACHIE.
PLEASE TAKE CARE OF MY , , and . PERHAPS NEXT WINTER WE CAN USE THEM WHEN WE play IN THE SNOW. Make SURE THAT YOUR MOTHER (MY WIFE) and puts MOTH BALLS IN THEM. How ARE YOUR . WERENT THE REPTILES NICE TO GIVE YOU THEIR OLD SKINS. WET KISSES TO THEE + thy SWEET MAMA-SAN.

Daddy
XXXXXX

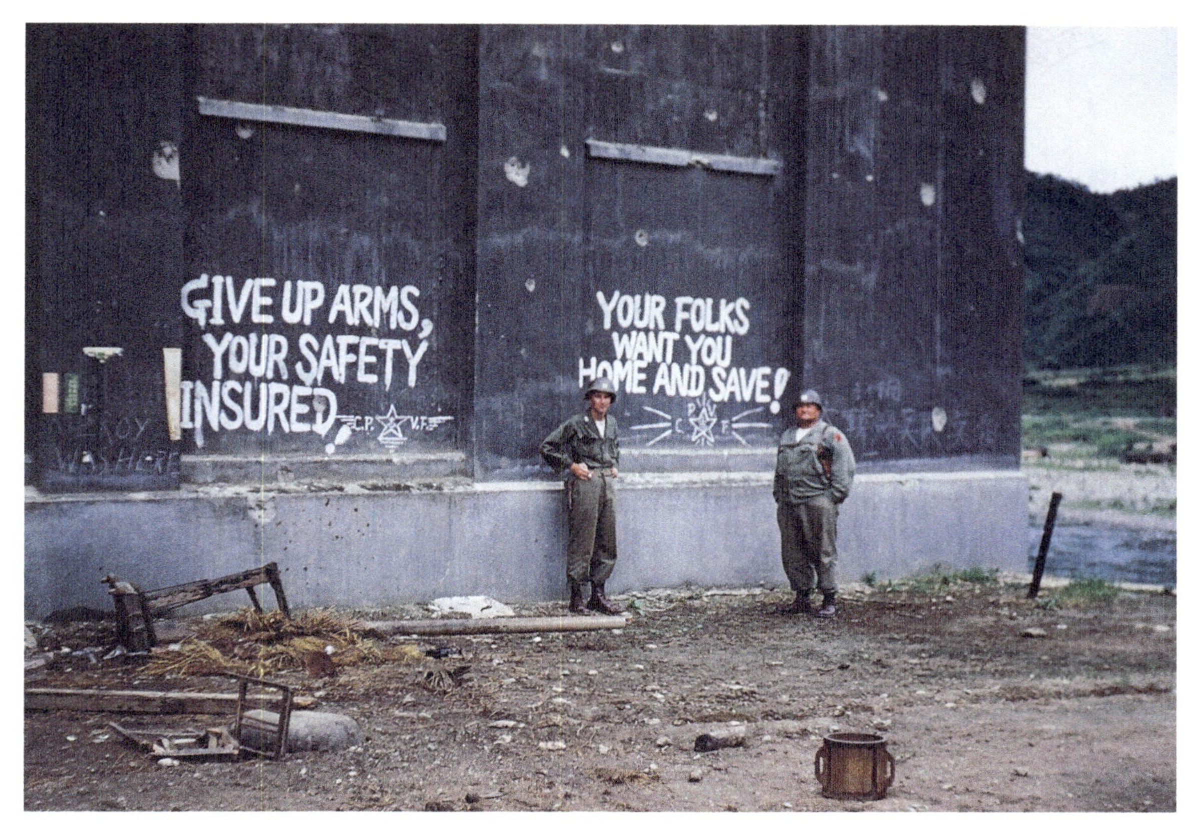

Capt. Hughes and Capt. Holms W. Underhill, Korea, 1950-51

CLEARING COMPANY
7TH MEDICAL BATTALION
APO 7 C/O PM SAN FRANCISCO, CALIFORNIA

June 4

Dear Ann —

Do you Read Chinese? If you do please tell me what this says. They drop these to the Chinamen from planes

C-47 with Speakers, Korea, Circa 1950-53, U.S. Air Force

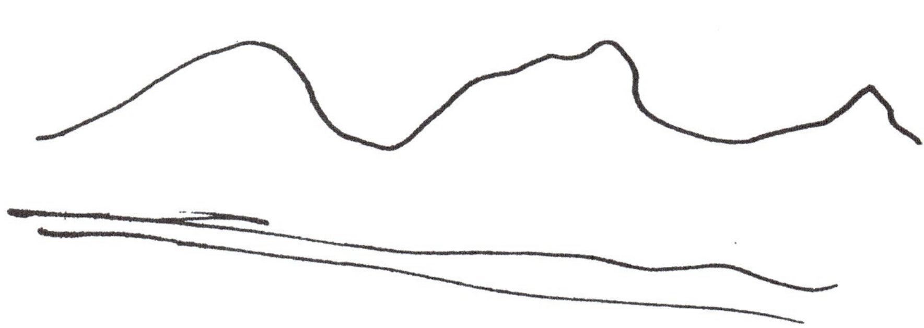

Love
Daddy
XXXXX

C-47s flew leaflet-drop/voice-broadcast sorties in late May, encouraging the enemy to surrender. Some 4000 enemy soldiers did surrender, with many carrying the dropped leaflets. The captives reported that there were morale problems in their units because of the UN aerial attacks.

Warnock, A. Timothy, Ed., "Air War Korea, 1950-53," *Air Force Association Online Journal*, Vol. 83, No. 10, Oct. 2000. Web. 25 Oct. 2012.

CLEARING COMPANY
7TH MEDICAL BATTALION
APO 7 C/O PM SAN FRANCISCO, CALIFORNIA

June 7, 1951

My Darling Sweet Annie;

Did you make medicines for sick people while you worked in the drug store? Did you make them right? I'll bet Mary K. wants you to work there all the time. You can take your pay in ice cream, candy, popsickles etcetera. Save some for me.

Love
Daddy
XXXXX

June 10

Dear Ann –

I want you to learn to take pictures so you can take some of your sweet mother to send to me.

Love
Daddy
xxxxx

June 12

Dear Ann –

WHAT IS YOUR SEAHORSE'S NAME? WHY DON'T YOU THINK UP SOMETHING SILLY?

LOVE!
Daddy
XXXXX

P.S. If you have been a good NON-pants-WETTING, BEDTIME HIGH AND DRY GIRL YOU CAN HAVE THESE KISSES I LEFT OUT ONE TIME.
XXXXX

June 15

Dear Annie

DO YOU HAVE SPOTS JUST WHERE YOU AREN'T TANNED OR EVERYWHERE?

Love
Daddy
xxxxx

June 17th

Dear Ann —

I have a little that every night he eats my CANDY. I am going to if he doesn't behave. How are your and I don't mean freckles. Can you yet. Can you take candy out of the air yet? When I get home we will play. O.K.? Now be a good girl. And don't make noise in. Give your mother a long kiss. Now have her kiss you right on the nose.

Love

Daddy
xxxxx

June 20, 1951

Dear Ann -

I USE MY RUBBER AIR MATTRESS TO RIDE DOWN THE RIVER JUST LIKE YOUR SEA HORSE.

Love
Daddy
XXXXX

AMERICAN RED CROSS

June 24

Dear Ann –

HAVE YOU LEARNED TO

DIVE INTO THE POOL YET?

LOVE

Daddy
xxxxx

CLEARING COMPANY
7TH MEDICAL BATTALION
APO 7 C/O PM SAN FRANCISCO, CALIFORNIA

June 26

Dear Annie —

DOES THIS HAPPEN TO YOU VERY OFTEN. I hope NOT.

LOVE
Daddy
XXXXX

CLEARING COMPANY
7TH MEDICAL BATTALION
APO 7 C/O PM SAN FRANCISCO, CALIFORNIA

June 29, 1957

Dear Ann -

When I come home will you teach me how to run the phonograph? You can play all your records for me. I will try to bring my rubber air mattress home so we can ride on the water. Won't that be fun. I hope you can swim by that time. Don't be afraid to duck your head ~~[illegible]~~ under the water. Do you tinkle in the pool when no one is looking, tsk, tsk, tsk. You'll ~~[illegible]~~ make all the fishies sick and give your sea horse a rash.

Be a good girl

Love

Daddy

xxxxx

CLEARING COMPANY
7TH MEDICAL BATTALION
APO 7 C/O PM SAN FRANCISCO, CALIFORNIA

Dear Ann - July 1, 1951

My air Mattress hit a nail yesterday and blew up. I am going to have a patch put on it.

Love
Daddy
xxxxx.

July 3rd

Daddy riding on the train – in his widdle room!
(hard to draw because train bumps around)

Peace talks begin
on July 8, 1951
but fighting continues.

July 11, 1951

Dear Ann

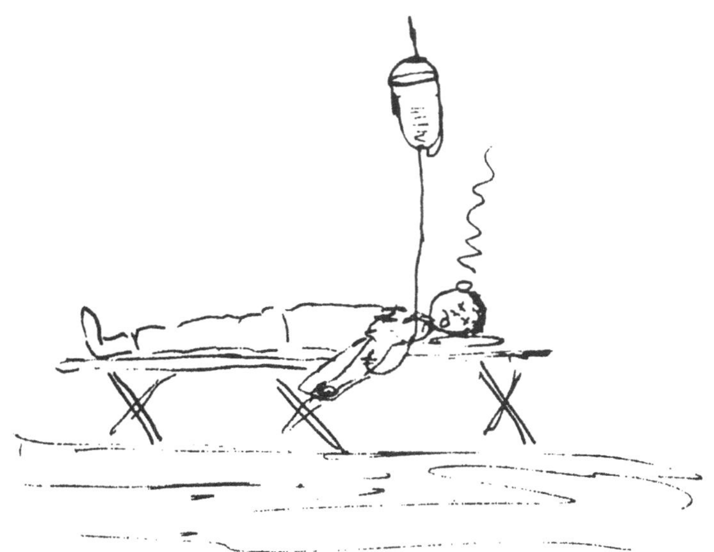

I was <u>so</u> sick the other day I had to eat sugar water + salt through my veins.

Love
Daddy
XXXXX

The cause of Captain Hughes' illness is unknown.

One of the medical surprises of the war, however, was the outbreak of epidemic hemorrhagic fever in 1951.

Ginn, Col. Richard V. N., *The History of the U.S. Army Medical Service Corps*, 1997, p. 243. history.amedd.army.mil. Web. 23 Sept. 2012.

It was treated with intravenous fluids.

Cowdrey, Albert, *The Medics' War*, p. 185.

July 15 xxx

Dear Annie -

I am sending you a picture I found in a magazine. Is this you? If it is where did you get the earings + pearls? I didn't know you wore lipstick. Write + tell me if this is you or not.

Love
Daddy
xxxxx

xxx

xx

xx

xxxx

For those stationed near a division headquarters, books and magazines were provided in squad tent dayrooms.

Cowdrey, Albert,
The Medics' War, p. 183.

Dear Ann:
19 July
Little Jap boy + Daddy.
wearing
clogg shoes

Geta Side View, Haragayato
en.wikipedia

The little boy is wearing clogs called geta.

Geta are a form of Japanese footwear that resemble both clogs and flip-flops. They are a kind of sandal with an elevated wooden base that can keep the feet dry in rain or snow. Geta make a noise similar to flip-flops, slapping against the heel whilst walking.

"Geta (footwear)," *en.wikipedia.org*. Web. 6 March 2013.

In July of 1951, one of the celebrities who provided entertainment to the troops in Korea was Jack Benny.

"U.S.O. History," *usoshows.co.uk*. Web. 17 March 2013. "Jack Benny on the 38th," *tralfaz.blogspot.com*. Web. 16 March 2013.

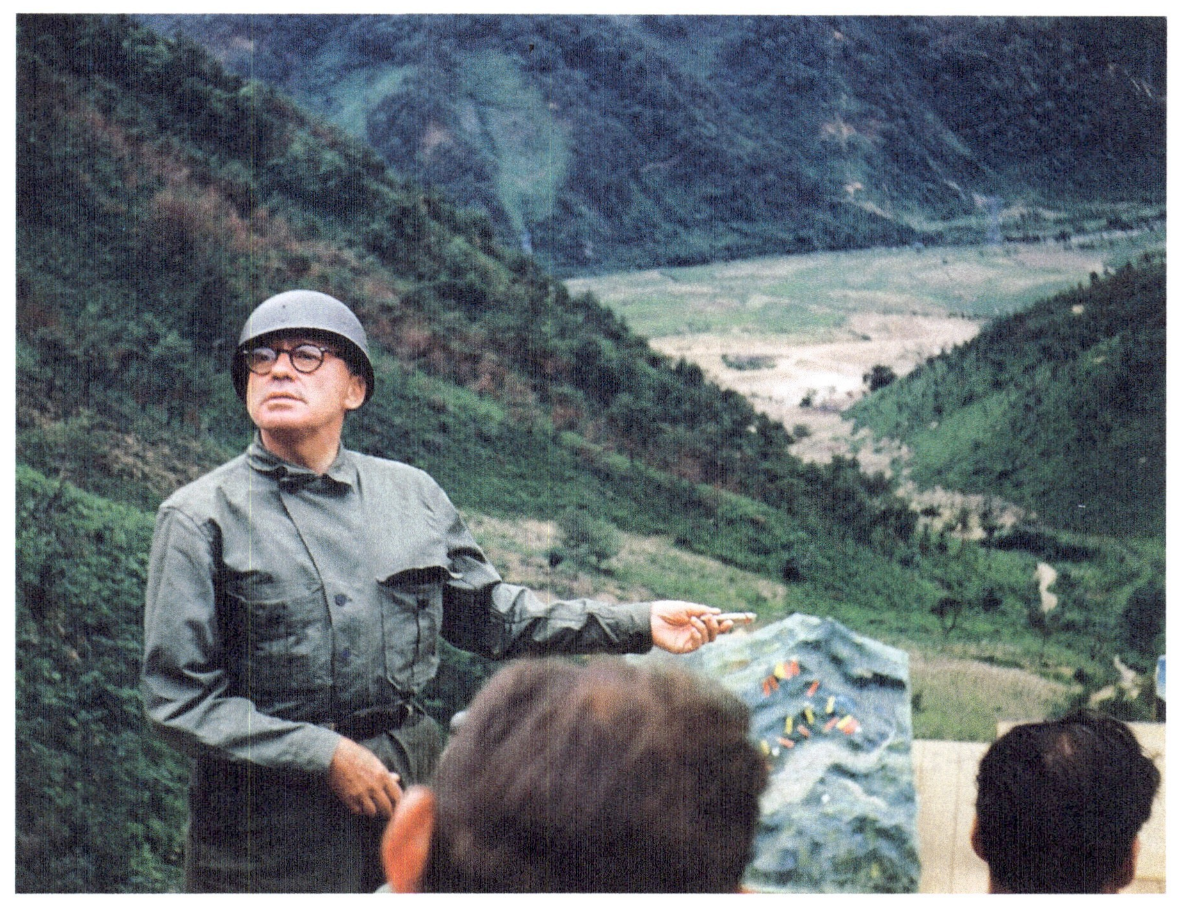

Comedian Jack Benny, Korea, 1950-51, Capt. John F. Hughes Photo

Dear Ann -

KEEP telling PEACHIE (THAT'S YOUR MOTHER) to GET A PROJECTOR SO YOU CAN SEE PICTURES.

LOVE
Daddy
xxxxx

Oxcart Traffic, Korea, 1950-51, Capt. John F. Hughes Photo

The Korean road traffic was predominantly by oxcart.

Appleman, Roy E., *South to the Naktong, North to the Yalu*, p. 0094. koreanwar2.org. Web. 17 Jan. 2013.

Even the best of the roads were narrow, poorly drained and surfaced only with gravel or rocks broken laboriously by hand.

Appleman, Roy E., *South to the Naktong, North to the Yalu*, p. 0093. koreanwar2.org. Web. 17 Jan. 2013.

July 24 '51

Dear Ann -

Road Rocks, Korea, 1950-51
Capt. John F. Hughes Photo

The korean boys carry big loads of Rocks on their Backs to put on the roads so they aren't slippery.

Love
John
xxxxx

7TH INFANTRY DIVISION

July 26 '51

Dear Ann -

Mosquito netting was used in all areas except the front lines, and chloroquine was issued to the men under the customary tight controls.

Cowdrey, Albert,
The Medics' War, p. 183.

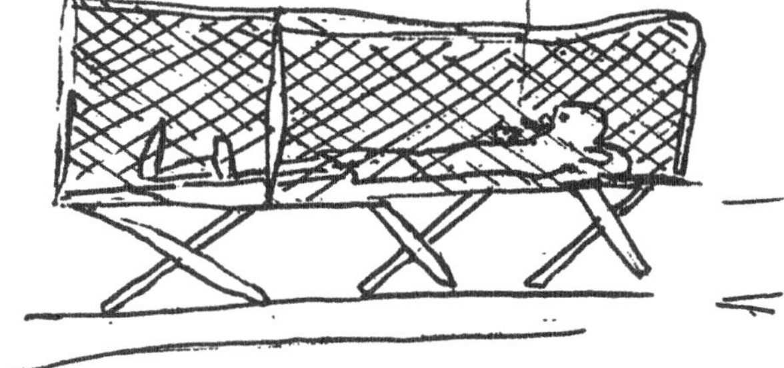

I SLEEP INSIDE A NET SO THE MOSQUITOES WON'T BITE ME ON THE SEAT.

Love
Daddy
XXXXX

Malaria was a constant threat in Korea because of a large civilian reservoir of the disease and the presence of anopheline mosquitoes.

Ginn, Col. Richard V. N., *The History of the U.S. Army Medical Service Corps*, 1997, p. 242. history.amedd.army.mil. Web. 23 Sept. 2012.

July 28, 1951

Dear Annie—

Why don't you write me soon. I want to know if you can swim yet. Did you get a rubber tube! I had a of you drawn in color but the artist forgot your pigtails. You look like your brother (when he comes) because he won't have pigtails. I am going to change my middle name to FOX? O.K.? We will call the little brother Bald Fox since he will have no hair. Do you think that is a good name for a boy. If we have a sister we can call her Red Fox if she has red hair like Nancy. Maybe we could change your name to Granny Fox. Tell me what you think

Love
Daddy
XXXXXXXXXXXXXXX

July 30, 1957

Dear [illegible] -

I have a hammock made OUT OF LITTER WHERE I TAKE a Nap EVERY afternoon

Love
Daddy
XXXXX

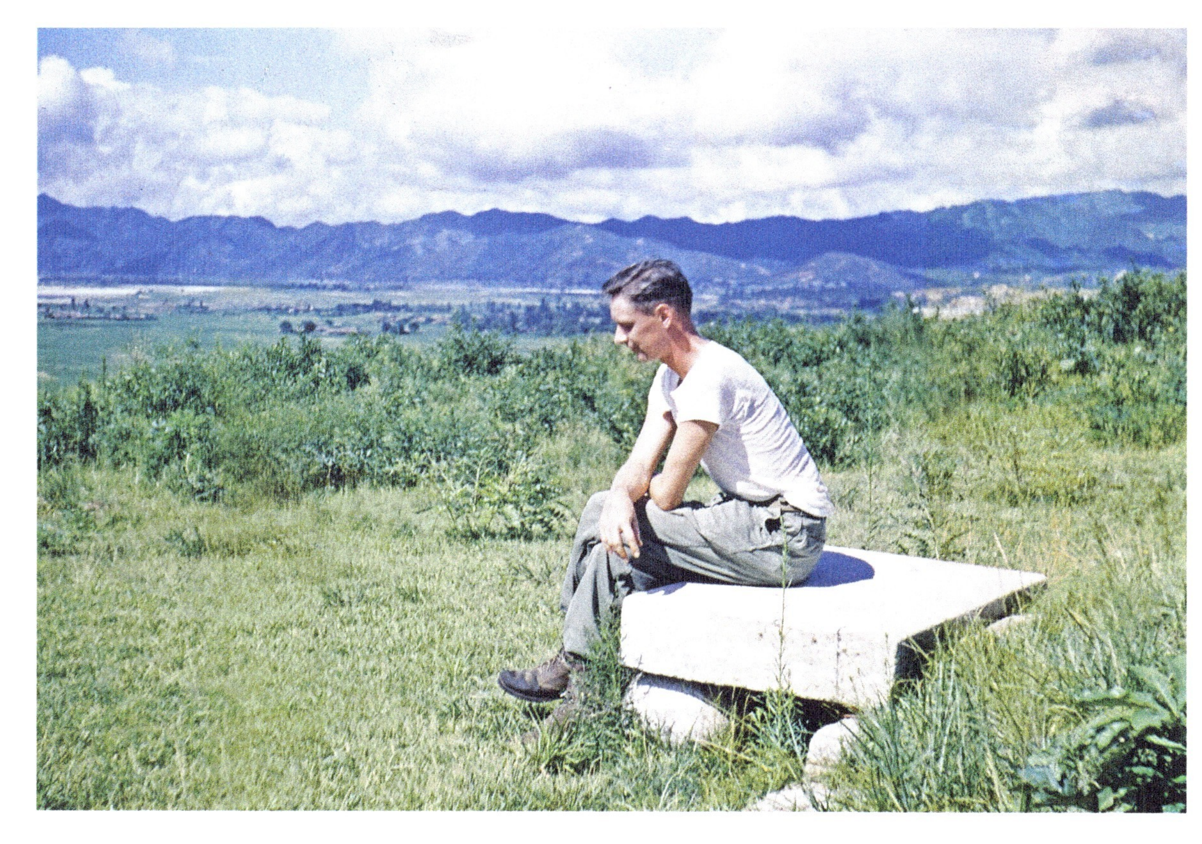

Capt. John F. Hughes, Korea, 1951

Aug 1, 1951

Dear Annie -

We gave a little Korean Boy a drink of whiskey yesterday. He didn't like it any more than you do.

Love
Daddy
XXXX

P.S. He made a funny face.

Aug. 5

Dear Annie—

I hear you eat  grapes when you go to market c̄ your grandfather (Bill). I don't want you to cry  when your mother goes out to play bridge. I don't like cry-babies. Be a good girl & I'll see you later.

Love

Daddy

XXXXX

Aug 7, 1951

Dear Annie

When I was a little boy I had an ear ache. Boy did it hurt. My mother took me too the Doctor. But he didn't have any Penicillin so it didn't go away for a long time.

Love
Daddy
xxxxx

Aug 8, 1951

Dear Ann —

Received your letter today. I am glad your [ear] isn't sore any more. Did they put penicillin in your seat  ? How do you like my pictures. Did Mama show you the "special picture."

Don't forget, you take a picture of your mother for me.

Love
Daddy
xxxx

Aug 12

Dear Annie

I have a little houseboy who is only as big as you are but who is 16 yrs old.

Love
Daddy
xxxxx

Aug 13 1957

Dear Ann -

Eye drops

Ear drops

Nose drops

Throat drops

WHEN DO YOU GET CHANCE TO SLEEP

Love
Daddy
xxxxx

Aug 16

PUT YOUR NICKELS IN THE PIGGY BANK SO WE CAN BUY A NEW CAR INSTEAD OF DRINKING SO MANY SODAS. OK GRANNY FOX?

LOVE

Daddy

XXXXX

CLASS OF SERVICE

This is a full-rate Telegram or Cablegram unless its deferred character is indicated by a suitable symbol above or preceding the address.

WESTERN UNION

1201

(50)

W. P. MARSHALL, PRESIDENT

SYMBOLS

DL=Day Letter

NL=Night Letter

LT=Int'l Letter Telegram

VLT=Int'l Victory Ltr.

The filing time shown in the date line on telegrams and day letters is STANDARD TIME at point of origin. Time of receipt is STANDARD TIME at point of destination

CTA097 1951 AUG 26 AM 10 02

CT.CZA090 INTL=0.SF SASEBO VIA RCA (357 358 43)=

EFM MARY L HUGHES=

744 MOHAWK ST COLUMBUS OHI

EXPECT TO BE HOME SOON DONT WRITE FURTHER. WILL CONTACT YOU ON ARRIVAL. LOVE AND KISSES=

JOHN=

No. Ga 1029 By To

THE COMPANY WILL APPRECIATE SUGGESTIONS FROM ITS PATRONS CONCERNING ITS SERVICE

Sept

U. S. S. GENERAL G. M. RANDALL AP-115

Dear Ann —

THIS IS ME RIDING IN A RICKSHAW.
JAPANESE BOY PULLS RICKSHAW. IN JAPAN
DADDY USES THIS INSTEAD OF A TAXI.

DADDY
XXXXXX

Oct 3

Dear Ann -

We have adopted a little girl. Her name is Su Wan. She is very thin since she hasn't had much to eat, but she is getting a Bawana Belly like you had once because all she does is eat. One of our cooks is feeding her.

Love
Daddy
XXXXX

> **"Most personnel stayed in Korea for just one year because it was known as a 'Police Action' and each of us earned points based on our assignment and the battles during which we served. Most personnel earned their rotation entitlement in 12 to 14 months."**
>
> Halbert, Doug, 7th Infantry Division Association re: 7th Medical Battalion, email to the editor, 23 Sept. 2012.

Korea, 1950-51, Capt. John F. Hughes Photo

CLASS OF SERVICE

This is a full-rate Telegram or Cablegram unless its deferred character is indicated by a suitable symbol above or preceding the address.

WESTERN UNION

1201

W. P. MARSHALL, PRESIDENT

SYMBOLS
DL=Day Letter
NL=Night Letter
LT=Int'l Letter Telegram
VLT=Int'l Victory Ltr.

The filing time shown in the date line on telegrams and day letters is STANDARD TIME at point of origin. Time of receipt is STANDARD TIME at point of destination

CTA102 OA072

O.SFP046 NL PD=MARTINEZ CALIF 13= 1951 SEP 14 AM 3 40

MARY L HUGHES=

744 MOTAWK STREET COLUMBUS OHIO=

ARRIVE CHICAGO 815 AM SUNDAY ON CHICAGO & NORTHWESTERN TRAIN 24 AT CHICAGO NORTHWESTERN STATION MEET ME AS ARRANGED=

JOHN=..

ec

GA1029

To	
By	At	To be

De-2-3850

THE COMPANY WILL APPRECIATE SUGGESTIONS FROM ITS PATRONS CONCERNING ITS SERVICE

Home

Bronze Star Medal

For his battlefield actions on October 9, 1950, Captain Hughes received a Bronze Star with a V-Device. The "V" stands for valor and denotes an award for heroism in a combat situation. He also received an Oak Leaf Cluster. This means that he twice was awarded the Bronze Star.

Oak Leaf Cluster Presentation to Captain Hughes

After returning to civilian life, Dr. Hughes, as many other veterans, spoke very little about what he personally had experienced during the war. His second child, John Robert, however, recalls that his Dad once told him that it was the greatest privilege of his life to have been able to serve and contribute to the Korean War effort - which now is so often referred to as "The Forgotten War."

Parties to the conflict
sign an armistice agreement
on July 27, 1953.

Saying Goodbye

Dr. Hughes practiced general medicine for several years after the war and then went into the field of psychiatry. He was mowing his lawn in Dublin, Ohio when he suffered a fatal heart attack on September 19, 1981. He was 59 years old. John Francis was survived by his wife, Mary, and their four children: Ann; John Robert; Molly and Richard.

Ann & Heidi
Portrait Courtesy of Photography by Ingrid

Ann grew up to be an artist. She married Dr. Paul Allen and had two children: Hilary and Caitlin. They lived in Massachusetts.

Ann loved every dog she ever had the opportunity to meet but particularly was enamored with boxers. Ann died in 2006 from complications of diabetes. She also was 59 years old at the time of her passing.

Acknowledgements

A big thank you goes to Jerry Piller and Doug Halbert of the Seventh Infantry Division Association for their assistance and help with the military vocabulary and history underlying "Letters to Ann."

Heartfelt thanks also go to the many family members who searched their memories and their attics to contribute to this wonderfully joint effort: Mary L. Hughes, John R. Hughes, Molly Kilb, Richard L. Hughes, Hilary Delage and Caitlin Connelly.

Any errors in the interpretation of the historical events or facts are solely my responsibility.

Ann Marie, *Editor*

Appendix

U.S. Army Center of Military History

Biographical Background

John Francis Hughes was born in Massachusetts on January 14, 1922.

1922

There was a wee bit of trouble in high school. His mother aptly noted that he could not have been in classes at Cambridge High and Latin and in the Boston Marathon on the same day. She drew this conclusion after opening up her daily newspaper and seeing her son in a marathon photo on the front page of the Boston Globe. Busted.

John attended Massachusetts State College from 1940 until 1943. Like so many patriotic young men of his era, he dropped out of college in his junior year to enlist in the World War II effort. He served with the Armed Forces as a hospital orderly at Nichols General Hospital in Kentucky until 1946.

That is where the lean, 6 foot, 155 pound, blue-eyed young man met Lt. Mary L. Schwartz of the U.S. Army Nurse Corps. Lt. Schwartz was a surgical nurse. They were a striking couple.

June 1945

Private Hughes and Lt. Schwartz

Mary, also known by her childhood nickname of "Peach," recalls that the two had to be very discreet about their dating because she outranked him. They were married on January 26, 1946.

Ann Isabel was the first of the couple's four children. She was born on December 20, 1946.

John resumed his studies at the University of Cincinnati. He obtained his medical degree in 1949. He then re-enlisted with the U.S. Army and was assigned to the 7th Infantry Division.

MEDICAL OFFICERS ARRIVE— Maj. Robert L. Rowan (center), chief of staff, 7th Infantry, welcomed eight medical officers to the 7th Infantry Division. The incoming officers are (left to right): Capt. John F. Hughes; Capt. Holms W. Underhill, Lt. Joseph C. Rodgers, Capt. William A. Whyland, Major Rowan, Lt. Leroy K. Norem, Capt. Joseph G. Ruhe, Lt. Robert E. Kreidinger and Capt. Stanley R. Lavietes. (**U.S. Army Photo**)

ENLISTED RECORD AND REPORT OF SEPARATION

19 12 11 ER/ 376493 HONORABLE DISCHARGE

1. LAST NAME - FIRST NAME - MIDDLE INITIAL	2. ARMY SERIAL NO.	3. GRADE	4. ARM OR SERVICE	5. COMPONENT
HUGHES HOHN F	11 080 462	PVT	MD	ERC

6. ORGANIZATION	7. DATE OF SEPARATION	8. PLACE OF SEPARATION
MED DETACH MICHOLS GEN HOSP	19 FEB 46	SEP CEN CAMP ATTERBURY IND

9. PERMANENT ADDRESS FOR MAILING PURPOSES	10. DATE OF BIRTH	11. PLACE OF BIRTH
22 SPRINGFIELD ST CAMBRIDGE MASS MIDDLESSEX CO.	14 JAN 22	SOMERVILLE MASS

12. ADDRESS FROM WHICH EMPLOYMENT WILL BE SOUGHT	13. COLOR EYES	14. COLOR HAIR	15. HEIGHT	16. WEIGHT	17. NO. DEPEND.
SEE # 9	BLUE	BRO	6'0"	155 LBS.	1

18. RACE: WHITE	NEGRO	OTHER (specify)	19. MARITAL STATUS: SINGLE	MARRIED	OTHER (specify)	20. U.S. CITIZEN: YES	NO	21. CIVILIAN OCCUPATION AND NO.
X				X		X		STUDENT COLLEGE X 02

MILITARY HISTORY

22. DATE OF INDUCTION	23. DATE OF ENLISTMENT	24. DATE OF ENTRY INTO ACTIVE SERVICE	25. PLACE OF ENTRY INTO SERVICE
	7 OCT 42	2 MAR 43	FORT DEVENS MASS

SELECTIVE SERVICE DATA	26. REGISTERED: YES	NO	27. LOCAL S.S. BOARD NO.	28. COUNTY AND STATE	29. HOME ADDRESS AT TIME OF ENTRY INTO SERVICE
		X			22 SPRINGFIELD ST CAMBRIDGE MASS.

30. MILITARY OCCUPATIONAL SPECIALTY AND NO.	31. MILITARY QUALIFICATION AND DATE (i. e., Infantry, aviation and marksmanship badges, etc.)
HOSPITAL ORDERLY 657	NOT AVAILABLE

32. BATTLES AND CAMPAIGNS

NONE

33. DECORATIONS AND CITATIONS

AMERICAN THEATER RIBBON; GOOD CONDUCT MEDAL; VICTORY MEDAL;

34. WOUNDS RECEIVED IN ACTION

NONE

35. LATEST IMMUNIZATION DATES: SMALLPOX	TYPHOID	TETANUS	OTHER (specify)	36. SERVICE OUTSIDE CONTINENTAL U. S. AND RETURN: DATE OF DEPARTURE	DESTINATION	DATE OF ARRIVAL
MAR 43	JUN 44	JUN 44	NOT AVAIL	NONE		

37. TOTAL LENGTH OF SERVICE — CONTINENTAL SERVICE: YEARS	MONTHS	DAYS	FOREIGN SERVICE: YEARS	MONTHS	DAYS	38. HIGHEST GRADE HELD
3	3	22	0	0	0	PVT

39. PRIOR SERVICE

NONE

FOR CONVENIENCE, A CERTIFICATE OF ELIGIBILITY NO 3352265 HAS BEEN ISSUED BY THE VETERANS ADMINISTRATION TO BE USED FOR THE FUTURE REQUEST OF ANY GUARANTEE OR INSURANCE BENEFIT UNDER TITLE III OF THE SERVICEMEN'S READJUSTMENT ACT OF 1944, AS AMENDED, THAT MAY BE AVAILABLE TO THE PERSON TO WHOM THIS SEPARATION PAPER WAS ISSUED. VAO-PORTLAND-ME

40. REASON AND AUTHORITY FOR SEPARATION

AR 615/365 CONVN OF GOVT DEMOBILIZATION

41. SERVICE SCHOOLS ATTENDED	42. EDUCATION (Years): GRAMMAR	HIGH SCHOOL	COLLEGE
NONE	8	4	2½

PAY DATA 28320

43. LONGEVITY FOR PAY PURPOSES: YEARS	MONTHS	DAYS	44. MUSTERING OUT PAY: TOTAL	THIS PAYMENT	45. SOLDIER DEPOSITS	46. TRAVEL PAY	47. TOTAL AMOUNT, NAME OF DISBURSING OFFICER
3	4	13	$ 200	$ 100	NONE	$ 49/95	217/32 BB CALLAWAY LT COL FD

INSURANCE NOTICE

IMPORTANT IF PREMIUM IS NOT PAID WHEN DUE OR WITHIN THIRTY-ONE DAYS THEREAFTER, INSURANCE WILL LAPSE. MAKE CHECKS OR MONEY ORDERS PAYABLE TO THE TREASURER OF THE U. S. AND FORWARD TO COLLECTIONS SUBDIVISION, VETERANS ADMINISTRATION, WASHINGTON 25, D. C.

48. KIND OF INSURANCE: Nat. Serv.	U.S. Govt.	None	49. HOW PAID: Allotment	Direct to V.A.	50. Effective Date of Allotment Discontinuance	51. Date of Next Premium Due (One month after 50)	52. PREMIUM DUE EACH MONTH	53. INTENTION OF VETERAN TO: Continue	Continue Only	Discontinue
X			X		FEB 46	1 APR 46	6/50	X	$	

54. RIGHT THUMB PRINT

55. REMARKS (This space for completion of above items or entry of other items specified in W. D. Directives)

ERC TIME FROM 7 OCT 42 THRU 1 MAR 43
NO DAYS LOST UNDER AW 107 LAPEL BUTTON ISSUED
ASR (2 SEP 45) 30

CM

56. SIGNATURE OF PERSON BEING SEPARATED	57. PERSONNEL OFFICER (Type name, grade and organization - signature)
John F. Hughes	J W NORTON 1ST LT INF — J W Norton

WD AGO FORM 53 - 55
1 November 1944

This form supersedes all previous editions of WD AGO Forms 53 and 55 for enlisted persons entitled to an Honorable Discharge, which will not be used after receipt of this revision.

MILITARY EDUCATION

14. NAME OR TYPE OF SCHOOL—COURSE OR CURRICULUM—DURATION—DESCRIPTION

WAS AN ARMY SPECIALIZED TRAINING PROGRAM STUDENT AT THE UNIVERSITY OF CINCINNATI, AT CINCINNATI, OHIO. FROM OCTOBER, 1945 UNTIL FEBUARY, 1946. TAKING A COURSE IN MEDICINE.

CIVILIAN EDUCATION

15. HIGHEST GRADE COMPLETED	16. DEGREES OR DIPLOMAS	17. YEAR LEFT SCHOOL
14½ YRS	NONE	1943.

18. NAME AND ADDRESS OF LAST SCHOOL ATTENDED

MASS. STATE COLL.
AMHERST, MASS.

19. MAJOR COURSES OF STUDY

AGRONOMY

OTHER TRAINING OR SCHOOLING

20. COURSE—NAME AND ADDRESS OF SCHOOL—DATE	21. DURATION

CIVILIAN OCCUPATIONS

22. TITLE—NAME AND ADDRESS OF EMPLOYER—INCLUSIVE DATES—DESCRIPTION

STUDENT COLLEGE;

ATTENDED MASSACHUSETTS STATE COLLEGE, AT AMHERST, MASSACHUSETTS. FROM SEPTEMBER 1940 TO MARCH, 1943. TAKING A COURSE IN AGRONOMY, COURSE CONSISTED OF SUBJECTS IN GENETICS, PHYSICS, CHEMISTRY, BOTONY ENGLISH, HISTORY, AND RELATED SUBJECTS. WAS STUDENT LIBRARIAN AND SL ALSO WORKED IN PLANT EXPERIMENTAL STATION. WAS A MEMBER OF THE VARSITY TRACK TEAM AND FRESHMAN BASEBALL TEAM.

OCT 8 1946
C.&R.-Rehab.
Veterans Administration
Cincinnati, Ohio

ADDITIONAL INFORMATION

23. REMARKS

WAS A MEMBER OF ROTC FROM 1940 TO 1942. IN THE CAVALRY RECEIVING BASIC TRAINING.

24. SIGNATURE OF PERSON BEING SEPARATED	25. SIGNATURE OF SEPARATION CLASSIFICATION OFFICER	26. NAME OF OFFICER (*Typed or Stamped*)
		E A HORN. 2ND LT AGD.

U. S. GOVERNMENT PRINTING OFFICE 16—45815-1

REPORT SYMBOL: (N) DD-1 N/A NOT APPLICABLE

REPORT OF SEPARATION FROM THE ARMED FORCES OF THE UNITED STATES

VBC

- CHARACTER OF SEPARATION: HONORABLE
- DEPARTMENT: ARMY
- 233777

SEPARATION DATA

- 1. LAST NAME - FIRST NAME - MIDDLE NAME: HUGHES JOHN FRANCIS
- 2. SERVICE NUMBER: 0 976 456
- 3. GRADE - RATE - RANK AND DATE OF APPOINTMENT: CAPT 26 JUN 50
- 4. COMPONENT AND BRANCH OR CLASS: AUS MC (SEE 38)
- 5. QUALIFICATIONS — SPECIALTY NUMBER OR SYMBOL: 3100; RELATED CIVILIAN OCCUPATION AND D. O. T. NUMBER: PHYSICIAN
- 6. EFFECTIVE DATE OF SEPARATION — DAY: 20; MONTH: JUN; YEAR: 52
- 7. TYPE OF SEPARATION: RELEASE FROM ACTIVE DUTY
- 8. REASON AND AUTHORITY FOR SEPARATION: EXPIRATION OF CATEGORY SR 135-175-5
- 9. PLACE OF SEPARATION: U.S. ARMY HOSPITAL, FT DEVENS, MASS
- 10. DATE OF BIRTH — DAY: 14; MONTH: JAN; YEAR: 22
- 11. PLACE OF BIRTH (City and State): SOMERVILLE, MASS
- 12. DESCRIPTION — SEX: MALE; RACE: CAUCASIAN; COLOR HAIR: BROWN; COLOR EYES: BLUE; HEIGHT: 5'11"; WEIGHT: 170

SELECTIVE SERVICE DATA

- 13. REGISTERED — YES / NO; SELECTIVE SERVICE NUMBER: N/A
- 14. SELECTIVE SERVICE LOCAL BOARD NUMBER (City, County, State): N/A
- 15. INDUCTED — DAY / MONTH / YEAR: N/A
- 16. ENLISTED IN OR TRANSFERRED TO A RESERVE COMPONENT — YES / NO; COMPONENT AND BRANCH OR CLASS: N/A; COGNIZANT DISTRICT OR AREA COMMAND: N/A

SERVICE DATA

ALL ENTRIES APPLY TO CURRENT PERIOD OF SERVICE (unless otherwise indicated)

- 17. MEANS OF ENTRY OTHER THAN BY INDUCTION: ☐ ENLISTED ☐ REENLISTED ☐ COMMISSIONED ☒ CALLED FROM INACTIVE DUTY
- 18. GRADE - RATE OR RANK AT TIME OF ENTRY INTO ACTIVE SERVICE: 1ST LT
- 19. DATE AND PLACE OF ENTRY INTO ACTIVE SERVICE — DAY: 26; MONTH: JUN; YEAR: 49; PLACE (City and State): HQ 1ST ARMY GOVERNORS ISLAND, N.Y.
- 20. HOME ADDRESS AT TIME OF ENTRY INTO ACTIVE SERVICE (St., R.F.D., County, City and State): 17 UNIVERSITY AVE, MEDFORD 55, MASS.

STATEMENT OF SERVICE FOR PAY PURPOSES	A. YEARS	B. MONTHS	C. DAYS
21. NET ( ) SERVICE COMPLETED FOR PAY PURPOSES EXCLUDING THIS PERIOD	-	-	-
22. NET SERVICE COMPLETED FOR PAY PURPOSES THIS PERIOD	2	11	25
23. OTHER SERVICE (Act of 16 June 1942 as amended) COMPLETED FOR PAY PURPOSES	3	5	12
24. TOTAL NET SERVICE COMPLETED FOR PAY PURPOSES	6	5	7

- 25. ENLISTMENT ALLOWANCE PAID ON EXTENSION OF ENLISTMENT, IF ANY — DAY / MONTH / YEAR / AMOUNT: N/A
- 26. FOREIGN AND/OR SEA SERVICE — YEARS: 1; MONTHS: 2; DAYS: 1
- 27. DECORATIONS, MEDALS, BADGES, COMMENDATIONS, CITATIONS AND CAMPAIGN RIBBONS AWARDED OR AUTHORIZED: ARMY OF OCCUPATION MED. W/JAPAN CLASP; KOREAN SV MED. W/5 BZ CAMP STARS; PRESIDENTIAL UNIT CITATION (ROK); MERITORIOUS UNIT COMMENDATION; BRONZE STAR MED W/"V" DEVICE AND OAK LEAF CLUSTER; GOOD CONDUCT MED; AMERICAN THEATER MED; WW II VICTORY MED.
- 28. MOST SIGNIFICANT DUTY ASSIGNMENT: MEDICAL OFFICER,
- 29. WOUNDS RECEIVED AS A RESULT OF ACTION WITH ENEMY FORCES (Place and date, if known): NONE
- 30. SERVICE SCHOOLS OR COLLEGES, COLLEGE TRAINING COURSES AND/OR POST. GRAD. COURSES SUCCESSFULLY COMPLETED: NONE; DATES (From—To): -; MAJOR COURSE: -
- 31. SERVICE TRAINING COURSES SUCCESSFULLY COMPLETED: NONE

INSURANCE AND PAY DATA

GOVERNMENT INSURANCE INFORMATION: IF PREMIUM IS NOT PAID WHEN DUE OR WITHIN THIRTY-ONE DAYS THEREAFTER, INSURANCE WILL LAPSE. MAKE CHECKS OR MONEY ORDERS PAYABLE TO THE TREASURER OF THE UNITED STATES. FORWARD PAYMENTS FOR N.S.L.I. TO THE COLLECTIONS UNIT, VA BRANCH OFFICE HAVING JURISDICTION OF AREA IN WHICH YOU MAINTAIN PERMANENT RESIDENCE. FORWARD PAYMENTS FOR U.S.G.L.I. TO COLLECTIONS DIVISION, VETERANS ADMINISTRATION, WASHINGTON 25, D. C. WHEN MAKING INSURANCE PAYMENTS BE SURE TO GIVE FULL NAME AND PERMANENT ADDRESS FOR MAILING PURPOSES, SERVICE SERIAL NUMBER AND POLICY NUMBER(S) IF KNOWN.

- 32. KIND OF INSURANCE (amount and premium due each month): $10,000 ($6.90); NONE
- 33. MONTH ALLOTMENT DISCONTINUED: JUN'52
- 34. MONTH NEXT PREMIUM DUE: JUL'52
- 35. TOTAL PAYMENT UPON SEPARATION: $1212.32
- 36. TRAVEL OR MILEAGE ALLOWANCE INCLUDED IN TOTAL PAYMENT: $16.02
- 37. DISBURSING OFFICER'S NAME AND SYMBOL NUMBER: R. PERKINS, MAJ, FC 215-494

AUTHENTICATION

- 38. REMARKS (Continue on reverse): BLOOD GROUP-'O'; REF 4-TEMP GR CAPT-AUS, PERM GR 1ST LT RES-MC, APTD - 3 JUN 49; DD FORM 217A (CERTIFICATE OF SERVICE) ISSUED.
- 39. SIGNATURE OF OFFICER AUTHORIZED TO SIGN: R W Lower
- NAME, GRADE AND TITLE (Typed): R. W. LOWER, Capt MSC, Ch, Pers Rec Br

PERSONAL DATA

- 40. V. A. BENEFITS PREVIOUSLY APPLIED FOR (Specify type) — COMPENSATION, PENSION, INSURANCE, BENEFITS, ETC.: EDUCATIONAL BENEFITS; CLAIM NUMBER: -
- 41. DATES OF LAST CIVILIAN EMPLOYMENT — FROM: 1945; TO: 1949
- 42. MAIN CIVILIAN OCCUPATION: PHYSICIAN (TRAINING)
- 43. NAME AND ADDRESS OF LAST CIVILIAN EMPLOYER: UNIVERSITY OF CINCINNATI, CINCINNATI, OHIO
- 44. UNITED STATES CITIZEN: ☒ YES ☐ NO
- 45. MARITAL STATUS: MARRIED
- 46. NON-SERVICE EDUCATION (Years successfully completed) — GRAMMAR: 8; HIGH SCHOOL: 4; COLLEGE: 9; DEGREE(S): MD; MAJOR COURSE OR FIELD: MEDICINE
- 47. PERMANENT ADDRESS FOR MAILING PURPOSES AFTER SEPARATION (St., R.F.D., County, City, and State): DIXFIELD, MAINE
- 48. SIGNATURE OF PERSON BEING SEPARATED: John F. Hughes

Stamp: Voucher No. 2608; Disb. Div.; Accts: H D Lloyd, Lt Col FC; Symbol Number 215-142

DD FORM 214

☆ G.P.O.: 1950-817007

INDIVIDUAL'S COPY
To Be Delivered To The Individual Being Separated

1

For those who served...

About the Editor

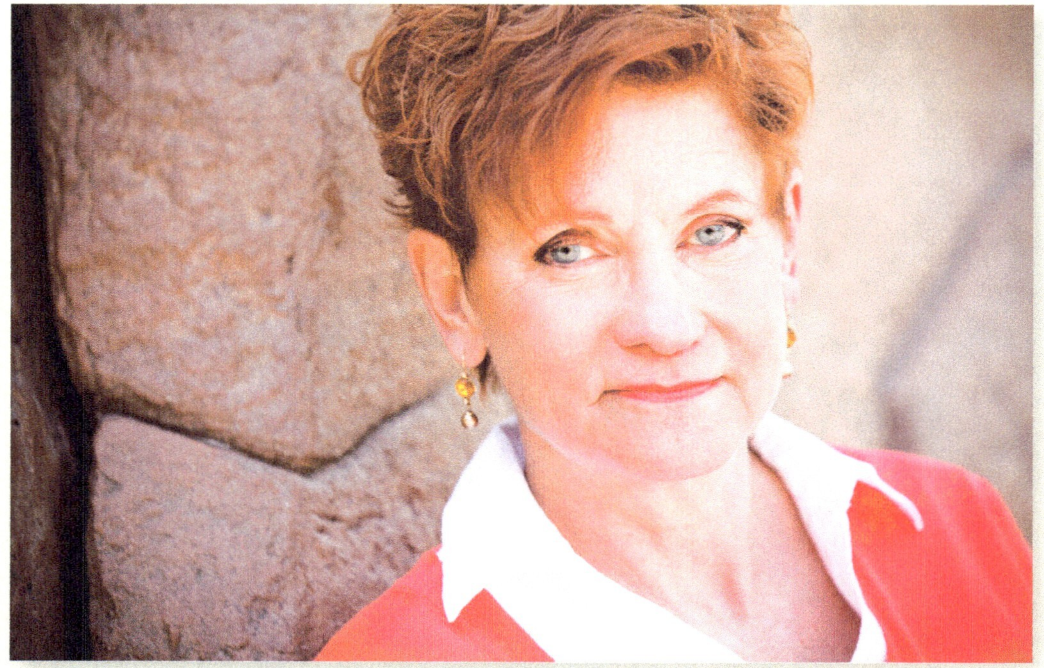

Photo by Lisa Seaman

Ann Marie started her professional career in the field of television journalism and then attended law school. She practiced as a trial litigation attorney before turning to editing. She is married to Neurologist Richard L. Hughes. They live in Denver, Colorado, where they ski and pretend to play golf. They have two children, Kristina A. Musial of Chicago and John T. Hughes of NYC.

Ann may be reached at annmarie83@mac.com.

CPSIA information can be obtained at www.ICGtesting.com
Printed in the USA
LVOW02*0110100114

368849LV00003B/8/P

9 780989 378802